# Titles available from boyd & fraser

## BASIC Programming

Applesoft BASIC Fundamentals and Style
BASIC Fundamentals and Style
Complete BASIC for the Short Course
Structured BASIC Fundamentals and Style for the IBM® PC and Compatibles
Structured Microsoft BASIC: Essentials for Business
Structuring Programs in Microsoft BASIC

## COBOL Programming

Advanced Structured COBOL: Batch and Interactive
COBOL: Structured Programming Techniques for Solving Problems
Comprehensive Structured COBOL
Fundamentals of Structured COBOL

## Database

A Guide to SQL
Database Systems: Management and Design

## Computer Information Systems

Applications Software Programming with Fourth-Generation Languages
Business Data Communications and Networks
Expert Systems for Business: Concepts and Applications
Fundamentals of Systems Analysis with Application Design
Investment Management: Decision Support and Expert Systems
Learning Computer Programming: Structured Logic Algorithms, and Flowcharting
Office Automation: An Information Systems Approach

## Microcomputer Applications

An Introduction to Desktop Publishing
dBASE III PLUS® Programming
DOS: Complete and Simplified
Introduction to Computers and Microcomputer Applications
Macintosh Productivity Tools
Mastering and Using Lotus 1-2-3®, Release 3
Mastering and Using Lotus 1-2-3®, Version 2.2
Mastering and Using WordPerfect® 5.0 and 5.1
Mastering Lotus 1-2-3®
Microcomputer Applications: A Practical Approach
Microcomputer Applications: Using Small Systems Software, Second Edition
Microcomputer Database Management Using dBASE III PLUS®
Microcomputer Database Management Using dBASE IV®
Microcomputer Database Management Using R:BASE System V®
Microcomputer Productivity Tools
Microcomputer Systems Management and Applications
PC-DOS®/MS-DOS® Simplified, Second Edition
Using Enable®: An Introduction to Integrated Software

## Shelly and Cashman Titles

Computer Concepts with Microcomputer Applications (Lotus 1-2-3® and VP-Planner Plus® versions)
Computer Concepts
Essential Computer Concepts
Learning to Use WordPerfect®, Lotus 1-2-3®, and dBASE III PLUS®
Learning to Use WordPerfect®, VP-Planner Plus®, and dBASE III PLUS®
Learning to Use WordPerfect®
Learning to Use Lotus 1-2-3®
Learning to Use VP-Planner Plus®
Learning to Use dBASE III PLUS®
Computer Fundamentals with Application Software
Learning to Use SuperCalc®3, dBASE III®, and WordStar® 3.3: An Introduction
Learning to Use SuperCalc®3: An Introduction
Learning to Use dBASE III®: An Introduction
Learning to Use WordStar® 3.3: An Introduction
BASIC Programming for the IBM Personal Computer
Structured COBOL: Pseudocode Edition
Structured COBOL: Flowchart Edition
RPG II, RPG III, & RPG/400

# PC-DOS®/MS-DOS®
## Simplified

### Second Edition

**ROD B. SOUTHWORTH**

**Laramie County Community College**

boyd & fraser publishing company

## CREDITS:

**Publisher:** Tom Walker
**Acquisitions Editor:** Jim Edwards
**Production Editor:** Pat Donegan
**Director of Production:** Becky Herrington
**Manufacturing Director:** Dean Sherman
**Composition:** Huntington & Black Typography
**Cover Illustration & Design/Book Design:** Becky Herrington

 © 1990 by boyd & fraser publishing company
A Division of South-Western Publishing Company
Boston, MA 02116

Manufactured in the United States of America

**DOS** is a registered trademark of IBM Corporation.
**MS-DOS** is a registered trademark of Microsoft Corporation.
**PC-DOS** is a registered trademark of IBM Corporation.

**Library of Congress Cataloging-in-Publication Data**

```
Southworth, Rod B., 1941-
    PC-DOS/MS-DOS simplified / Rod B. Southworth. -- 2nd ed.
        p.   cm.
    ISBN 0-87835-460-3
    1. PC DOS (Computer operating system)  2. MS-DOS (Computer
operating system)   I. Title.
QA76.76.063S66   1990
005.4'46--dc20                                          89-22377
                                                           CIP
```

3 4 5 6 7 8 9 10 E 4 3 2 1 0

# CONTENTS

# PREFACE

*T*his book is ideally suited for use in any formal educational or training environment, or for self-study. **PC-DOS/MS-DOS Simplified, Second Edition** was developed with the one-credit PC-DOS/MS-DOS course in mind, but is equally appropriate for use as a supplementary text in any course that introduces DOS commands. Even though no previous experience with computers is required in order to use this book, students who typically gain the most from it are those who have already experienced frustration when trying to use DOS effectively.

## OBJECTIVES OF THIS BOOK

The objectives of this book are as follows:

- To provide readers with a fundamental overview of the components of microcomputer systems.
- To introduce readers to the concepts of using an operating system.
- To simplify the use of high-frequency DOS commands and associated options.
- To improve readers' overall ability to use microcomputers effectively through minimized keystrokes, improved disk management, and customized execution of computer processes.

## DISTINGUISHING FEATURES

### Simplifies Using DOS

In order to accommodate the different backgrounds and expertise of students using this book, topics in this text are developed in a logical step-by-step manner. By building on students' prior experience and carefully constructed examples of DOS in action, this simplified approach helps readers become self-sufficient microcomputer users.

### Focus on High-Frequency DOS Commands

This textbook features step-by-step instruction in using the DOS commands and associated options that are most frequently required by microcomputer users. It is designed to help readers gain better understanding and control of microcomputers through efficient use of DOS.

### Floppy Disk vs. Hard Disk Environments

In keeping with the current trend in microcomputer instruction, this book consistently addresses using DOS in both floppy disk and hard disk environments. Using DOS with floppy disk systems and hard disk management is presented in complete detail.

### Emphasis of DOS Structure

An overall understanding of the structure of DOS is essential in effective computer use. This text's thorough coverage of disk organization and management teaches readers to effectively utilize the computer system with increased efficiency.

### Class-tested Exercises

Each chapter includes a substantial set of student exercises that have been class-tested over the last two years. These exercises build on material learned from previous chapters, as well as reinforcing the new material contained in each chapter. These exercises are specifically designed for floppy disk systems, but can be easily modified for hard disk systems.

### Actual Screen Illustrations

Each DOS instruction is fully supported with screen "dumps" that accurately reflect what users' screens will look like as they execute each target command. The screen illustrations provide users with visual verification, which highlights the impact of each operation performed.

### Proven Material

The evolution of this text is based on many semesters of teaching this course and on the collective experience of the instructors and students who have shared their comments and suggestions. Every attempt has been made to preserve the integrity of those elements that proved effective and to improve on those that did not.

### Instructor's Support Material

An Instructor's Manual featuring additional student exercises, helpful teaching suggestions, answers to chapter review questions, and a selection of class-tested, multiple choice test questions is available for use by adopters of this text. Instructors may contact South-Western Publishing Company to obtain this supplementary material.

## ACKNOWLEDGMENTS

This book would not have been possible without the guidance, help, and advice of many supportive individuals. First and foremost, I would like to thank all who contributed to the tremendous success of the first edition of **PC-DOS/MS-DOS Simplified**. Without your support, this second edition would not have been possible. To Bill Gardner, Southern Technical College; Jean E. Gutman, University of Southern Maine; Gary A. Lombardo, University of Southern Maine; Michael Michaelson, Palomar College; Joel Richards, Southern Technical College; and Paul Ross, Millersville University; I offer my sincere thanks for providing valuable criticism and suggested improvements during each phase of the book's development. I wish to thank all of the instructors and students at Laramie County Community College who had faith in my material and never failed to make valuable comments about whatever they did and did not like. The entire staff at boyd & fraser, and especially Pat Donegan and Jim Edwards, did a remarkable job of editing and producing this text. To all of these people, I remain indebted for their efforts on my behalf.

To Devin, who spread warmth and love to everyone he touched, God bless you.

Rod B. Southworth
Cheyenne, Wyoming                                                        October, 1989

# Chapter

# 1

# INTRODUCTION TO MICROCOMPUTERS

**HARDWARE**

☐ The Central Processing Unit (CPU)
Bits, Bytes, and Words
Input/Output Devices
Secondary Storage

**SOFTWARE**

☐ Application Software
System Software

# 1

# INTRODUCTION TO MICROCOMPUTERS

*A*fter reading this chapter, you should understand the major components of microcomputer systems. Because students using this text undoubtedly have varying degrees of computer experience and knowledge, this chapter provides an opportunity to reach a common framework of microcomputer concepts and terminology.

All microcomputer systems are comprised of two major parts: hardware and software. This chapter discusses each of these parts to bring students to a minimal level of understanding about microcomputer systems. This basic system knowledge should greatly facilitate both the learning and understanding of either PC-DOS or MS-DOS.

When you purchase a microcomputer system, you may need to make choices about the power of the CPU and the types of input, output, and storage devices you will want to attach. The level of technical knowledge presented in this chapter will assist you in making the right choices.

# HARDWARE

☐

Typically, discussion of **hardware** involves three categories: the central processing unit (CPU), the various input/output (I/O) devices, and storage devices. Figure 1-1 summarizes the various hardware parts and categories of microcomputer systems discussed in this chapter.

*Figure 1-1*

*Microcomputer Hardware*

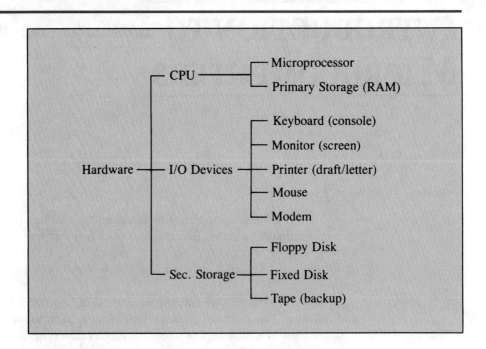

## The Central Processing Unit (CPU)

The **central processing unit**, or **CPU**, has often been described as the "heart" of a computer system. It is comprised of a **microprocessor** and a varying amount of temporary storage locations referred to as **primary storage**. The CPU is typically organized around one of four microprocessor chips designed by Intel Corporation: the 8088, 8086, 80286, and 80386. Each of these microprocessor chips has different capabilities, related primarily to speed and overall processing power. Soon, microcomputers will utilize the most powerful microprocessor chip, the Intel 80486.

# Bits, Bytes, and Words

All computer circuits, including microprocessors, function in one of two states: on or off. Symbolically, we represent the on condition by the value 1 and the off condition by the value 0. These two values are binary digits, or **bits**. A grouping of bits can be combined to represent characters that we need to store data on a computer. Eight bits are typically grouped together to represent characters, where a character is a number (0–9), alphabetic letter (A–Z), or special symbol such as an asterisk, dollar sign, decimal point, and so on. For example, the bit pattern 10000001 might represent the letter A.

When each group of 8 bits is individually addressable it is called a **byte**. Most of the earlier computers were "byte machines." However, it is generally more efficient to access and work with more than one character at a time. When bytes are grouped (always in multiples of 2), the addressable groups are called **words**. A 16-bit word represents 2 characters, a 32-bit word represents 4 characters, and so on. Word machines access and transfer characters faster than byte machines.

The 8088 microprocessor is the most common of the four chips. It has a 16-bit internal word structure with an 8-bit path for transfer of input and output data. The 8086 is a similar chip, but with a 16-bit path for input and output, which allows for faster transfer of data between the CPU and I/O devices.

All microprocessor chips use a **clock rate** that determines the frequency of the internal operations and keeps everything in proper synchronization. The faster the clock runs, the faster the computer can process data and instructions. Clock rates are measured in units called **megahertz**, a term for one million cycles per second. The internal clock speed of both the 8088 and 8086 chips is 4.77 megahertz (MHz).

The 80286 microprocessor has a 32-bit internal word length with a 16-bit I/O path. Its internal clock is rated at 8–12 MHz, making it at least twice as powerful as the older, more common chips previously mentioned. The 80386 microprocessor is at least twice as fast as the 80286 with an internal clock speed of 16–33 MHz. The processing power of the 80386 is often required for the high-powered graphics used in desktop publishing or computer-aided design (CAD) applications. But don't get discouraged if you don't have the latest chip. The more common chips used today, while not as fast and powerful as the 80386, are more than adequate for most applications. As my Dad once told me, "When the speed limit is only 55 MPH, a VW bug can be as effective as a fancy sports car."

Primary storage, the second major part of a CPU, is a temporary holding location for both programmed instructions (software) and data to be processed.

The number of primary storage locations on microcomputers typically ranges from 256KB to 768KB, where KB is roughly equivalent to a **kilobyte,** or 1000 characters. Actually, one KB of storage is 1024 bytes, but it is a lot simpler to work in units of 1000. The microprocessor is responsible for executing software instructions that tell the computer how to process the data in primary storage. These instructions also tell the microprocessor when and where to send data to an output device, such as a printer, as well as when and where to get additional data to be processed.

Primary storage is generally referred to as **RAM (Random Access Memory)** because the storing of data causes the affected storage locations to be changed and allows for any storage location to be accessed at any time. Characters are stored in a given storage location and remain there until new characters have replaced them, or until the electricity has been turned off. Because most RAM chips lose their "memory" when the power is discontinued, primary storage is considered temporary. If you want to permanently save data, you must save it to a secondary storage device such as magnetic tape or disk.

It is important for microcomputer users to realize the potential damage that static electricity can do to the sensitive electronic circuits in the CPU. The amount of static electricity that you sometimes feel when you touch a doorknob or another person is hundreds of times greater than the static electricity needed to permanently damage a microprocessor or RAM chip. For this reason, precautions should be taken to minimize the potential for static electricity around your microcomputer. The computer or computer area can be protected by the following techniques:

- Place the computer system in a noncarpeted area.
- Keep the computer area at a relative humidity of about 45% or more.
- Use a static spray on fabrics.
- Use a static mat and good grounding to discharge static electricity.

## Input/Output Devices

Input/output devices are the means by which you enter data into the computer (input) or view data you have previously saved (output). This chapter discusses the most common devices: keyboard, monitor, printer, mouse, and modem.

## The Keyboard

The **keyboard** on a personal computer is an input device similar to a typewriter keyboard, except it has additional special keys. The IBM-PC and IBM-compatible keyboards typically have between 84 and 104 keys (see Figure 1-2) and vary somewhat among manufacturers. Most variation occurs in the number and placement of special keys provided. The cost of most keyboards is about $100. A good understanding of the keyboard is essential when working with DOS.

**Figure 1-2**

*Typical Keyboards*

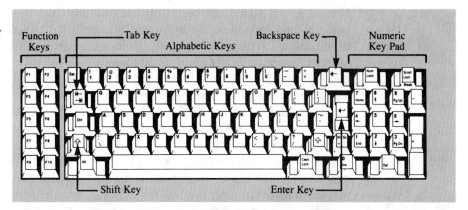

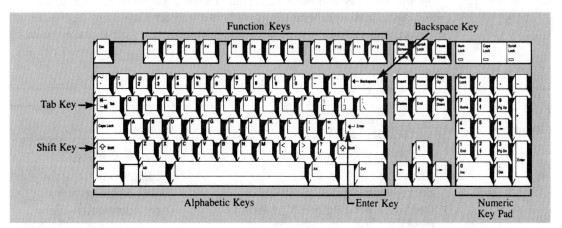

A set of 10 keys, usually on the left side (or additional top row) and labeled F1 through F10, are called **function keys**. These "programmable" keys serve different functions depending on how the software has been programmed to use them. When a function key is referred to in this text or in the DOS Manual, it will generally be called by the key name, such as the F1 key or the F6 key. When you are instructed to enter the F6 function key in the text exercises, it will be shown as < F6 >.

The **numeric keypad** is a group of 10 keys, usually located near the right side of the keyboard, containing keys numbered 0–9. The keypad can be used to enter numbers only when the Num Lock key has been activated. The Num Lock key is an example of a "toggle" key, one that acts as a switch. Press it once and the toggle is switched on; press it a second time and it is turned off. Normally, the Num Lock key is off and you enter numbers by pressing the numeric keys located on the top row of the keyboard. Another example of a toggle key is the Caps Lock key that shifts all lowercase alphabetic characters (a–z) to uppercase (A–Z) when switched on.

With the Num Lock key switched off, the numeric keypad keys become arrows that are used to position the cursor on the screen. The cursor is a special character, usually a blip or an underline, that identifies a location on the computer screen where the next action or entry of data is to occur.

Some keys must be used in combination with other keys to obtain the desired results. With the exception of the numeric keypad, all keys with both an upper and lower character shown on the key require that the Shift key be pressed to enter the upper symbol. For example, in order to enter a $, you must press the Shift key and the 4 key simultaneously. The Shift key is also used to enter capitalized alphabetic letters without using the Caps Lock key. Some of the more important keys used in combination and their functions are shown in Figure 1-3. On some keyboards the Break key is shown as the Scroll Lock key.

*Figure 1-3*
*Combination Keys*

| Combination Keys | Function |
| --- | --- |
| Control + Break (Ctrl-Brk) | Break execution |
| Control + S (Ctrl-S) | Pause screen |
| Shift + Print Screen (Shift-PrtSc) | Print current screen |
| Control + Print Screen (Ctrl-PrtSc) | Print continuous screen |
| Control + Alt + Del (Ctrl-Alt-Del) | System reset (warm boot) |

As you enter commands from a keyboard, you can use the Backspace key, normally shown as a large left-facing arrow (←), to backspace and erase unwanted characters. The Backspace key erases one character at a time each time it is pressed.

Once a command has been keyed completely, it must be sent to the computer, or entered, by pressing the **Enter key**. The Enter key, sometimes shown as the Return key, is normally located near the right side of the keyboard, just to the left of the numeric keypad. On most keyboards it is shown as a bent left-facing arrow (↵). We refer to this key as the Enter key in the rest of the text. Figure 1-4 summarizes the keyboard keys.

*Figure 1-4*
*Summary of*
*Keyboard Keys*

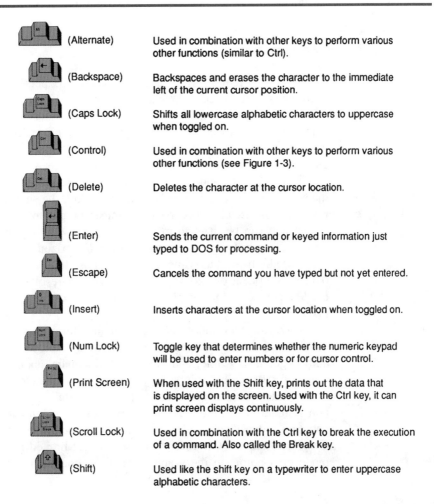

(Alternate)   Used in combination with other keys to perform various other functions (similar to Ctrl).

(Backspace)   Backspaces and erases the character to the immediate left of the current cursor position.

(Caps Lock)   Shifts all lowercase alphabetic characters to uppercase when toggled on.

(Control)   Used in combination with other keys to perform various other functions (see Figure 1-3).

(Delete)   Deletes the character at the cursor location.

(Enter)   Sends the current command or keyed information just typed to DOS for processing.

(Escape)   Cancels the command you have typed but not yet entered.

(Insert)   Inserts characters at the cursor location when toggled on.

(Num Lock)   Toggle key that determines whether the numeric keypad will be used to enter numbers or for cursor control.

(Print Screen)   When used with the Shift key, prints out the data that is displayed on the screen. Used with the Ctrl key, it can print screen displays continuously.

(Scroll Lock)   Used in combination with the Ctrl key to break the execution of a command. Also called the Break key.

(Shift)   Used like the shift key on a typewriter to enter uppercase alphabetic characters.

Since modern keyboards are electronic and not mechanical, a very light touch is all that is required to activate the keys. If you continue to hold down a key, the keyboard will repeat that keystroke until you release the key. This is known as the repeating key concept and may cause problems for you until you get used to it.

In computer terminology, a **buffer** is a holding area that can temporarily store a limited number of computer characters. The keyboard has a buffer that allows it to retain keystrokes until the program you are using has "caught up" with you. If you are an extremely fast typist or are using a program that processes keystrokes slower than you are entering them, the buffer can save them until they are needed. As you type, some keystrokes will not be automatically "echoed" on the screen, since they may still be in the buffer.

### The Monitor

In addition to requiring the use of a keyboard, personal computers need a **monitor** (screen) to communicate with the user. Keystrokes entered at the keyboard are displayed on the screen to provide visual verification. When the computer needs to communicate with you, it normally displays data, error messages, and system prompts on the screen. Most monitors can display 80 characters of text on a line and 25 lines on the screen.

The sharpness and clarity of images on the screen are directly related to the screen resolution. The higher the resolution, the sharper the image. Screen resolution is usually rated by the number of picture elements (pixels) on a screen that can be lit to form images. Low-resolution monitors display about 320 × 200 pixels on the screen, 320 pixels horizontally and 200 pixels vertically. Medium-resolution monitors, like most IBM-PCs, typically have either 640 × 200 pixels or 720 × 350 pixels. Higher-resolution monitors, like those used by engineers for complex computer graphics, go as high as 1024 × 1024 pixels.

There are two major categories of monitors: monochrome monitors and color monitors. Monochrome monitors are limited to a single color, usually amber, green, or white, and are suitable for many applications. If an application requires multiple colors or graphics, a color monitor is required.

In order for a monitor to be able to communicate with the CPU, a control unit is required. These control units are called **video display adapters**. Two common video display adapters are the monochrome adapter and the Color Graphics Adapter (CGA). A CGA monitor is limited to 16 colors in the text mode or 4 colors in the graphics mode of operation. For this reason, CGA video display adapters are being replaced with more powerful adapters, such as the EGA or VGA card. The EGA card (Enhanced Graphics Adapter) can generate up to 64 colors. To display up to 256 colors, use a VGA (Video Graphics Array) display adapter. The cost of a medium-resolution color monitor with an EGA card is about $500; the cost of a high-resolution monitor with a VGA card is about $1000.

### *The Printer*

Printers for microcomputers are generally classified as one of two types: letter quality or draft quality (dot matrix). **Letter-quality printers**, which print documents that look as if they were created by a typewriter, typically create each character by striking a fully formed image of a character against an inked ribbon and paper. **Draft-quality printers**, which produce images of lesser quality but are sufficient for most applications, use a dot matrix technique that creates a pattern of dots to represent each character or image. Many dot matrix printers can produce near letter-quality output by reprinting each character, adding additional dots to fill in the image with a denser pattern of dots. The printing of additional dots tends to cut printing speeds by half or more. As a general rule, dot matrix printers are faster and less expensive than letter quality printers. In addition, dot matrix printers are more flexible in that they can print a wide variety of patterns, including graphics.

Printers for microcomputers typically print 80 characters per line, but by printing in condensed mode they can print 132 characters on a line. Prices for printers vary greatly due to the wide range of capabilities, but a fairly typical printer sells for about $300 and prints 120 characters per second.

The latest type of dot matrix printer is the **laser printer**, which uses a toner process similar to the common copy machine. Laser printers have extremely high quality print, handle graphics well, are quite fast, and cost about $2000. These are becoming very popular for business and desktop publishing applications using microcomputers.

### *The Mouse*

Most microcomputers allow a **mouse** to be attached as an input device. The mouse is a pointing device. As you move the mouse across a flat surface, it relays information to the computer that moves the cursor in the direction you move the mouse. Once the curser is positioned, you can press a button on the mouse to inform the computer you have selected the desired spot on the screen.

A mouse allows you to select options on the screen quickly and easily. However, you need software, called a mouse driver, that supports a mouse before you can use it to control the cursor. A typical mouse with its supporting software costs about $100.

### The Modem

To communicate with other computers via telephone lines, two items are required: a **modem** (at each end) and compatible communications software. A modem is used to convert the computer's digital signals to the analog signals used by telephones, and vice versa. Modems can be internal (located inside the computer) or external. The speed with which the modem can send and receive data is known as its **baud rate**. The higher the baud rate, the less time it takes to transmit and receive data. Common baud rates are 1200 and 2400, but data can be transmitted at a rate as high as 9600 baud. If you divide the baud rate by 10, you can approximate the data transmission rate in more relevant terms, characters per second.

Communications software is readily available to let you use your modem effectively. The major purpose of communications software is to guide you through the various communications parameters required to let your computer talk to another computer. In addition to the baud rate, communication parameters include the specific bit patterns for transmission and the methods of error detection and correction. A 1200-baud modem with supporting software generally costs between $100 and $200.

### The I/O Interface

Any input/output device attached to a CPU must have some type of control unit to allow it to interact with the CPU and make the appropriate translations between each I/O device and the CPU. These control units are often referred to as **interface boards** or **cards**. They consist of a sturdy card containing electronic chips. Occasionally, static electricity or some other power-related problem causes these chips to fail and they may have to be replaced.

These cards are relatively easy to remove because they plug directly into slots on the CPU's system board. The system board is the large printed circuit board that holds most of the computer chips that make up the CPU. The chips on the system board include the microprocessor, RAM chips, and ROM chips. The number of slots available (sometimes called expansion slots or option slots) depends on the system board. Most system boards have slots for one keyboard, a monitor (display screen adapter), two serial devices (like a mouse or a modem), a parallel device (like a printer), and two or more disk drives. These slots are all connected to a common communications channel called a bus. The bigger the bus, the faster data can be transmitted inside the CPU. The bus on most microcomputers is either an 8-bit or a 16-bit path.

Slots for a variety of serial and parallel devices are referred to as ports. Data is transmitted through a serial port via a single wire one bit at a time. The most common serial port is based on an industry standard called the RS-232 serial interface. It is designed for a wide variety of uses. Since each character requires 8 bits of data, serial transmission is not very fast. Considerably faster transmission speeds are obtained with a parallel port. These ports use 8 parallel wires to send data 8 bits at a time.

Because the number of slots is limited, manufacturers have developed multifunction boards, which combine two or more tasks. Some of the functions typically combined on multifunction boards include additional primary storage, a clock and battery to automatically set the computer's clock, a parallel port to connect a printer, several RS-232 ports to connect serial devices like a mouse or modem, and a game adapter port to connect a joystick.

## Secondary Storage

When you create data on a computer or write programs, you cannot save them permanently in RAM, the computer's primary storage area. RAM is not large enough to store even a modest number of files containing data and/or programs. Secondary storage facilities are required to store a potentially unlimited amount of data on a permanent basis. The costs per bit stored on secondary storage are considerably less than for storage in primary storage. Microcomputers usually support three types of secondary storage devices: floppy disks, hard (or fixed) disks, and magnetic tape.

### *Floppy Disks*

**Floppy disks** are the most common medium for secondary storage and come in various sizes. The most common size for the IBM-PC family of personal computers is 5 1/4-inch disks, each of which can contain up to 360KB (or 360,000 characters) of data. These disks allow data to be written on 40 tracks per side, using both sides for storage. Some 5 1/4-inch disks, called high-density disks, can hold up to 1,200,000 bytes (1.2 megabytes) of data. (A **megabyte**, MB, is equivalent to about one million characters.)

When you insert a floppy disk into a floppy disk drive and close the latch, the disk is secured by two clamps that close on the largé center hole of the disk. When data is to be either read from or written to the disk, a motor connected to the clamps spins the disk inside its protective jacket at 300 RPM, about 10 times faster than a 33 1/3 album spins on a record turntable. A small red light on the disk drive indicates when the drive is spinning, so you will know not to attempt to remove the disk. The smaller 3 1/2-inch disks use improved technology to record 720KB of data. DOS Version 3.2 supports these newer disks, but the older versions do not.

Floppy disks are not completely reliable because they can be damaged. However, if you take proper care of them, floppy disks can serve you faithfully for a long time. Figure 1-5 contains some helpful and important tips for the "care and feeding" of floppies.

***Figure 1-5***

*Proper Care of Floppy Disks*

1. Store floppies in their protective covers when not in use.
2. Store them vertically to minimize chances of warping.
3. Shade them from direct sunlight or intense heat.
4. Write on any attached labels with felt tip pens only.
5. Never touch the recording surface of a floppy disk.
6. Never bend, fold, or otherwise mutilate a floppy disk.
7. Keep the disk clean from contaminants, including smoke.
8. Do not attempt to clean the surface of a disk.
9. Never place a disk near a magnetic field or magnets.

### Hard Disks

Hard disks, sometimes referred to as fixed disks because they are not removable, have a significant advantage over floppy disks in that they are roughly 20 times faster to use. When the hard disk drive is operating, it spins at 3600 RPM, or 12 times faster than a floppy disk. In addition, you do not have to be continually swapping disks, since hard disks will typically hold 20, 40, or even

191 megabytes of data. Hard disks can store data using a much higher density than floppy disks because they use rigid metal platters in a sealed environment. A 20MB hard disk can store the equivalent of 56 360KB floppy disks.

It is not practical for personal computers to have only a hard disk drive installed, however. Floppy disks are used extensively for transferring data and programs from one computer to another and for backup, so it is ideal to have at least one hard disk drive and one floppy drive. In addition, because of the vast number of files that can be stored on most hard disk systems, it is important to establish appropriate file naming conventions, a topic covered in Chapter 2.

### *Magnetic Tape*

Another medium of secondary storage is **magnetic tape**. Since this medium only allows for sequential retrieval of data, it is not appropriate for most applications. Magnetic tape is significantly less expensive than disks (per unit stored), so it makes an ideal medium for storing historical or backup data. Large businesses typically use one of their expansion slots on the system board to connect a high-speed tape drive to be used solely for backup. A fast, high-capacity tape drive that greatly facilitates backup costs about $400.

# SOFTWARE
☐

In addition to hardware, a computer system must have software to control and operate the hardware. Figure 1-6 outlines the various classifications of software required.

**Figure 1-6**
*Microcomputer*
*Software*

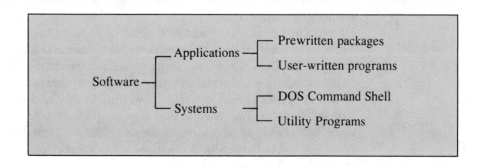

## Application Software

**Application software** is written for a specific purpose, such as inventory, word processing, or payroll. It can be created by the user at great expense and time or it can be purchased outright. Novice users should not attempt to write their own application software; it takes a great deal of skill to be able to write reasonably productive software. Furthermore, the cost of prewritten programs is relatively cheap.

Individual application programs are more helpful if they are **integrated** — in other words, provide several applications in one package. Integration provides two major benefits. Learning how to operate the programs is easier, since commands are usually similar in integrated packages. In addition, it is easier to transfer data between a variety of integrated applications. For example, you can easily transfer data from a spreadsheet to your word processor.

## System Software

Your computer system needs **system software** to act as an interface between the application programs and the hardware. The two major functions of a computer's operating system are to control the computer's operations and to manage files. The operating system allows you to use the computer in either an interactive mode or a batch mode. In normal **interactive processing**, the user enters a command, the computer executes that command, and then the user issues another command when the computer has finished the previous one. **Batch processing** occurs after a user has stored a file of commands. The user can direct DOS to automatically execute the commands in the file one after another. This text is devoted to the operating system used by the IBM and IBM-compatible family of microcomputers (PC-DOS and MS-DOS) and covers both methods of operation.

System software is generally thought of as being both a **command shell** and a set of supporting **utility programs**. The command shell for the IBM-PC family is PC-DOS. Even with all its power and capabilities, many users have found the need for additional software, primarily to assist them in making DOS friendlier (easier to use) and more powerful, so they turn to utility programs like PC-Tools or Treeview. Most utility programs are devoted to improving upon DOS, such as Microsoft Windows, Norton Utilities, and Fastback, to name just a few. Appendix B discusses utility support programs and provides more detailed examples.

The last topic that we should mention before delving into DOS is a special kind of software called firmware. **Firmware** is defined as software contained in the form of hardware. This hardware, used to store preprogrammed instructions, is called **ROM (Read-Only Memory)**. Special-purpose programs are built into ROM chips during manufacturing. Because programs stored in ROM are permanently embedded into computer memory, they are available to be executed without having to be specifically loaded into RAM. ROM is a form of nonvolatile memory in that it does not lose its instructions when the power is turned off, like RAM. Therefore, ROM is often used to hold operating system startup programs and language translators such as BASIC.

When you turn on your computer system, a ROM chip automatically tests the hardware for problems and then loads a portion of DOS from the default disk drive. If you have an IBM-PC (not one of the many IBM clones or IBM compatibles), the instructions for interpreting BASIC programs are contained on a proprietary ROM chip. In the future, more software will be available in the form of inexpensive ROM chips. Currently, laptop and other portable microcomputers contain both the operating system and several common application programs in ROM.

# *Review Questions*

1. What are the two major parts of a microcomputer?
2. What is the major difference between primary storage and secondary storage?
3. What is the major difference between RAM and ROM?
4. What is the purpose of a clock rate in a microprocessor?
5. What is the potential danger of static electricity?
6. What is the purpose of function keys?
7. What is meant by the term "toggle key"?
8. Give two examples of toggle keys on the keyboard.
9. What keys must be pressed to halt execution of an operation?
10. What happens when you press the Backspace key?
11. What is the repeating key concept?
12. What term is used to define the sharpness and clarity of images on the display screen?

13. What is the difference between a "byte machine" and a "word machine"?
14. What are some advantages that dot matrix printers have over letter-quality printers?
15. What is the most common form of secondary storage on microcomputers?
16. What are the major differences between hard disks and floppy disks?
17. What is the difference between application and system software?
18. What are the major benefits of utility support programs?
19. What is the difference between batch and interactive processing?
20. What are the benefits of using integrated software packages?

# *Chapter*

# 2

# INTRODUCTION TO DOS

## BASIC DOS FUNCTIONS
☐ Control of Input/Output Operations
Interpret and Execute Commands
File Management

## SAVING FILES WITH DOS
☐

## BOOTING DOS
☐

## FUNDAMENTAL DOS COMMAND CONCEPTS
☐ Default Disk Drive
Standard Device Names
File Naming Conventions
Wildcard Characters
The DOS Directory Listing
Internal vs. External Commands
DOS Versions

## FORMATTING DISKS WITH DOS
☐

# 2

# INTRODUCTION TO DOS

*T*he primary objective of Chapter 2 is to teach you the basic functions of DOS related to file management and command processing. By the end of this chapter, you will understand such file management techniques as how disks are formatted and how files are saved on disk. In addition to how to boot DOS, Chapter 2 also teaches you fundamental DOS command concepts including the default disk drive, standard device names, file naming conventions, wildcard characters, and internal vs. external commands. This chapter introduces you to four introductory DOS commands: DATE, TIME, DIR, and FORMAT.

An **operating system** is an integral part of all computer systems. It allows users like yourself to conveniently use the computer as a tool. For example, suppose you wanted to use your computer to create a term paper with a new word processing program you recently acquired. You would have to know how to load and execute the correct application program. In addition, that application program has to know how to save and retrieve disk files on your computer. This is all provided for you by your computer's operating system.

The operating system is a necessary translator between the hardware and either application programs or users, coordinating and controlling all the activities of the computer (see Figure 2-1). The operating system contains a group of commands and programs that allow users to interact directly with the computer. For example, it provides an easy way to copy data from one disk to another, allowing you to conveniently make backup copies of important data.

---

**Figure 2-1**

*The Role of an Operating System*

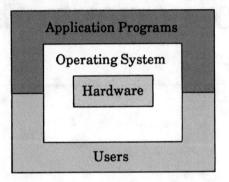

This chapter introduces you to a specific type of disk operating system (DOS) called PC-DOS (or MS-DOS) that is used on both IBM and IBM-compatible microcomputers. Many users are confused by the terms PC-DOS and MS-DOS. Essentially, the two operating systems are identical. PC-DOS is the IBM implementation of DOS and MS-DOS is Microsoft's version used on all IBM-compatible microcomputers. Because of the similarities of PC-DOS and MS-DOS, this text refers to this operating system simply as DOS. When a specific reference is needed, the appropriate term will be used.

## BASIC DOS FUNCTIONS

DOS has three major functions. The first controls the input and output operations of your computer. The second function interprets and executes commands that you enter from your keyboard or other input devices. The third major function deals with file management, which allows you to permanently record files on disks and manage them effectively.

## Control of Input/Output Operations

All application programs share the same input and output problems. They all have to accept data from the keyboard, display data on the monitor, store data temporarily in main memory, store data permanently on disk, and retrieve data from disks. It requires a great number of instructions to coordinate and control all these activities on a microcomputer. Without an operating system, each application program would have to duplicate these instructions. On the PC-DOS disk, two "hidden files," **IBMDOS.COM** and **IBMBIO.COM**, provide the input/output instructions required by DOS and by application programs. They are called hidden files because they do not appear on the directory of files when you attempt to list the files contained on your DOS disk. IBMDOS.COM provides some common services like copying files, deleting files, searching directories, and accepting keystrokes from the keyboard. IBMBIO.COM contains additions and corrections to the basic I/O system routines that are built into your system on ROM chips. In MS-DOS, the hidden files are named **MSDOS.SYS** and **IO.SYS**.

## Interpret and Execute Commands

The command processor part of DOS interprets and executes the commands that you enter and interprets and executes commands from application programs as well. Without an operating system, you would have no effective way to communicate with the hardware and direct its activities.

## File Management

As a user, you are heavily involved with the file management role of DOS. For example, before files can be saved on a disk, you must prepare the disk to record files. Then you can save, rename, copy, or delete disk files. DOS provides a series of complex commands to allow both the user and application programs to manage the multitude of disk files that you create over a period of time. Subsequent chapters of this book are primarily devoted to the file management commands provided by DOS.

# SAVING FILES WITH DOS

☐

A **file** is a group of related records, where each **record** consists of a string of characters that can be entered and saved as part of that file. Records consist of either program instructions or data. Thus, files are categorized as either **program files** or **data files**.

Saving files on disk is a requirement of all operating systems. The files you create and work with in main memory are temporary and only become permanent when you save them on disk. When you turn off the computer or otherwise lose power to main memory, all programs and data stored in main memory are destroyed. However, you can easily save files on disk and recall them when needed. DOS saves files when directed to by application programs. You can also save files by using the COPY command, which is covered in detail later.

Although it appears a fairly simple process, DOS goes through a number of important steps to save files. The following overview will help you understand this process.

(1) IBM and IBM-compatible floppy disk drives are double-sided, meaning data can be stored on both sides of the disk. The area on formatted disks used to record data is comprised of clusters that are in turn made up of **sectors** and **tracks**. A **cluster** is the smallest addressable location that can save data on a disk. The cluster size on a 360KB floppy is 1024 bytes, since a sector contains 512 bytes and two sectors (one on each side of a disk) make a cluster. Although the sector size remains constant, the size of the cluster may vary depending on the disk drive used and the number of read/write heads per track. On stacked hard disks, cluster sizes typically involve 4 sectors or 2048 bytes. Large cluster sizes improve performance of disk access when files are large, but may waste space when files are smaller than a cluster.

By recording both sides of a disk before moving to another track, recording head movement is minimized and disk access speed is increased. When you issue a save command from an application program or directly from DOS, the operating system reads the directory portion of the disk to determine a suitable location to save the file.

(2) If the file being saved is a new file, DOS tries to locate enough unallocated space (clusters) to hold the file. If the file was previously saved on that disk, DOS replaces the old file with the contents of the file currently in main memory. Because DOS uses whatever clusters it can find to save the data, the clusters may not be adjoining. Files written in noncontiguous clusters are called **fragmented files**. The additional head movement caused by fragmentation may slow down the reading and writing of these files considerably.

(3) When a file has been saved, DOS updates the **File Allocation Table (FAT)** on the disk with the clusters required to permanently store the file. Then it updates the directory on the disk with the size of the file in bytes and the date/time the file was saved. For this reason, it is important that the operating system is booted with the correct date and time. Depending on the type of disk, the directory allows up to 512 entries, including filenames and subdirectory names. Since subdirectories are normally applicable to hard disk systems, we discuss them in Chapter 7. The file information stored on a disk directory is as follows:

- **filename and filename extension**
- **file attribute (hidden file, read-only file, and backup status)**
- **date and time of creation or last update**
- **starting cluster number in FAT**
- **file size in bytes**

# BOOTING DOS
☐

Before you can use an operating system, you must load it from a secondary storage device such as a disk to the main memory of the computer. Because not all of the operating system can be loaded at once, a process known as **booting** the system is used to load the controlling portion of the operating system.

There are two general methods of booting any operating system. One way is called a "**cold boot**" because the computer is turned off prior to booting the operating system. The second method is termed a "**warm boot**" because the computer is already warmed up and was previously in use, but needs to be rebooted. In both cases, DOS executes the same sets of commands in the boot process.

The major difference between the two ways of booting the system is in how the boot process is initiated. In a cold boot, the computer is simply turned on to initiate the booting process. In the warm boot, you must enter a sequence of three keys simultaneously: the Control key, the Alternate key, and the Delete key (**Ctrl-Alt-Del**). It is advisable to use a warm boot whenever you can to minimize the possibility of damaging the electronic chips when the power is turned on.

To do a cold boot of DOS from a floppy disk, follow these steps:

(1) Place the disk containing DOS in Disk Drive A with the latch securely closed. Drive A is usually the top drive or leftmost drive in microcomputers with two drives. Then turn on the power to both the monitor and the CPU.

(2) The microcomputer begins executing a small startup program stored in ROM that instructs it to run some predetermined diagnostic tests. These tests include checking the computer's RAM and keyboard interface to make sure they are functional. If there are any problems, the program displays an appropriate error message on your screen.

(3) If the computer passes the diagnostic checks, the program in ROM loads the two DOS hidden files contained on the DOS disk in Drive A. It also loads the file called COMMAND.COM into RAM from Drive A. **COMMAND.COM** contains many of the DOS commands you will use. It is the primary command interpreter, processor, and loader. Occasionally, another program requires some of the memory occupied by the COMMAND.COM file. When that program is finished, you will be prompted to insert the disk containing the COMMAND.COM file in the default drive so that it can be reloaded.

(4) At this point, DOS also looks for an optional **CONFIG.SYS** file that can be used to specify some of the different ways your system can be configured, or customized. In addition, DOS accommodates more advanced users by looking for a file on Drive A called **AUTOEXEC.BAT**. If DOS finds this file, it executes it immediately. Sophisticated DOS users utilize an AUTOEXEC.BAT file to simplify the booting process by executing a common set of boot-related programs. The use of these two files are explained in later chapters.

(5) If there is no AUTOEXEC.BAT file, the system asks you to enter the correct date and correct time, so that it can keep track of the time with its own internal clock. Once you have entered the date and time, DOS displays the version number of the operating system and prompts you to enter a command. The **default prompt** is A>, where the A represents the **default disk drive**, the one containing DOS. Figure 2-2 shows you how the screen might look if you entered a date of July 4, 1990 and a time of 1:45 p.m. The A> is the system prompt, which requests the next command; the underline character following it is the cursor. For illustrative purposes, the data you entered is shown in boldface.

*Figure 2-2*

*Screen Display
after Booting
PC-DOS*

Current date is Tue 1-01-1980
Enter new date (mm-dd-yy): **07-04-90**
Current time is 0:01.05.58
Enter new time: **13:45**
The IBM Personal Computer DOS
Vers. 3.10 (C)Copyright International Business Machines 1981, 1985
            (C)Copyright Microsoft Corp. 1981, 1985
A>_

The system date is entered using month, day, and year in the form of mm-dd-yy or mm/dd/yy. You can use either a slash (/), a hyphen (–), or a period (.) to separate the date entries.

The system time is entered using hours, minutes, seconds, and hundredths of seconds in the form of hh:mm:ss:xx. The use of seconds (ss) and hundredths of seconds (xx) is optional. Hours are always entered using the 24-hour system and range from 0 to 23. You can only use the colon (:) or a period (.) to separate time entries.

As with most operating systems, when you are finished entering a command or some data, like date or time, you need to press the Enter key to let the system know you are finished keying.

If at a later time you wanted to change either the system date or time, all you would need to do is enter a simple command. To change the date, enter **DATE** and press the Enter key. DOS displays the current date for you and asks you to enter a new date. The format of the new date is the same as with the boot process (mm-dd-yy). When entering the date, you do not have to enter leading zeros. For example, the month of February can be entered as 02 or just 2. Also, you do not have to enter the century. For instance, the year 1990 is simply entered as 90. If you change your mind and decide not to change the date, just press the Enter key.

To change the time, enter **TIME** and change it using the same format as the boot process. For all practical purposes, you only need to enter the hours and minutes (hh:mm). When entering hours, remember that hours are entered using the 24-hour system. For example, 8:15 p.m. is entered as 20:15.

As long as DOS keeps running, it keeps track of the time, automatically changing both the time and the date. Many systems today have a small battery and additional software to keep track of the date and time when the computer is turned off. When the system is booted, an AUTOEXEC.BAT file can contain the command to automatically set the system date and time from this battery-operated clock.

The boot process is identical for hard disk systems except for one major difference: DOS looks for the DOS boot files on the hard disk rather than on a floppy disk drive.

# FUNDAMENTAL DOS COMMAND CONCEPTS

Before learning specific DOS commands, you should understand the basic concepts common to the majority of DOS commands. Once learned, these concepts can be easily applied to all the individual commands. The concepts to be learned include the use of a default disk drive, standard device names used by DOS, the need for effective file naming conventions, the use of wildcard characters, and the basic types of DOS commands.

## Default Disk Drive

Most computer systems have at least two disk drives. Applications on floppy disk systems generally require that the program disk be located in one drive and your data disk in another. If your computer has only one floppy disk, it will likely have a hard disk as well. A hard disk can easily contain both your application program(s) and your data. However, you would still need a floppy disk drive to allow you to load files from floppy disks to the hard disk or to make backup copies of your hard disk files on floppy disks.

When running DOS, the system needs to know what disk drive applies to the commands you enter. DOS employs the "default drive technique," a concept that is referred to often in this text. Fundamental to this concept is that you can specify which of the disk drives is to be the default. Whenever you enter a command that does not contain a disk drive specification, DOS substitutes the default drive for the missing one(s) in the command. By understanding the default drive concept when entering commands, you can save a significant number of keystrokes. Remember, you only need to designate a disk drive if it is other than the default drive.

To identify the different disk drives, DOS uses a coding scheme consisting of letters: A and B are used for floppy drives, C and D are used for hard disk drives. DOS establishes the initial default drive as the drive that was used to boot the system. You can easily change the default to another drive whenever you wish. When you booted DOS and saw the A> prompt, the A referred to the default disk drive. The > is the symbol used by DOS to identify the system prompt. This is the operating system's way of reminding you what drive is the current default drive.

To change the default drive, you need to enter a new disk drive letter followed by a colon. For example, the command **B:** entered at the A> prompt changes the default drive from A to B. Once entered, the default drive is the B drive (the second floppy drive) and the system prompt is displayed as B>.

## Standard Device Names

As with most operating systems, DOS reserves some names to represent system devices. For example, when used in DOS commands, the reserved word **CON** represents the keyboard (console). The reserved words **LPT1** and **PRN** are used to designate the line printer. Printer designations are especially useful when you wish to redirect output that would normally go to the screen to the printer for a hard copy listing. Because reserved words have specific meaning to DOS, you should never use them to name a file. Other reserved device names include AUX1 and COM1 (serial port 1 devices), COM2 (a serial port 2 device), LPT2 and LPT3 (parallel ports), and NUL (a nonexistent device).

## File Naming Conventions

DOS uses the **full filename** to tell it where to search for a specified file. The full filename consists of four parts: the disk drive designator, the path, the filename, and the filename extension. Only the filename itself is required. The optional parts are shown in brackets as follows:

```
[d:][path]filename[.ext]
```

The first part of the full filename, **[d:]**, is used to specify the disk drive. To specify a drive, enter the drive letter followed by a colon. If you omit the **drive designator**, the default disk drive is substituted by DOS.

The next part, **[path]**, is the location of the subdirectory containing the file. Discussion of this parameter is postponed until Chapter 7, when we discuss in detail hard disk systems that typically use subdirectories.

DOS requires that a **filename** be at least one character in length, but it can be as long as eight characters. Filenames can be made up of numeric digits, alphabetic letters, and certain special characters. You should avoid using any of the special characters, except possibly the hyphen (-), which is used to make filenames more readable. But don't use spaces or punctuation such as periods, commas, colons, or semicolons.

The final part is an optional extension. The **extension** is comprised of the same set of characters that are valid for filenames, but is limited to three characters. If an extension is used, it must be preceded by a period. Example: **A:JONES89.DOC**.

The intended purpose of a filename extension is to indicate the category of each file. Using filename extensions is highly recommended to aid in keeping track of your files. For example, you should use .DOC, .WP, or .TXT for word processing files and .WK1 or .WKS for worksheet files. Extensions can be very beneficial when used in conjunction with the wildcard characters discussed in the next section.

When creating filenames, you should always use meaningful titles to further classify the type of data contained in each file. You can code a great deal of information into your filenames. For example, a set of memos on the new bottling plant could be named BOTTLE1.DOC, BOTTLE2.DOC, etc. Or, if the memo dates were critical, the set could be named BOTmmdd.DOC, where the mm represented the month created and the dd the day. Later you will see how wildcard characters can be used to selectively work with only the desired category of files. When sorted file directories are displayed, the memos appear listed together in chronological sequence. As the number of your saved files grows, the benefits of care and foresight in creating filenames should become more significant.

When you assign file extensions, you should abide by the standard extensions already established and commonly used. Some of these standard extensions are described in Figure 2-3.

**Figure 2-3**

*Standard Filename Extensions*

```
$$$ – scratch or temporary file
BAK – backup file
BAS – BASIC program file (needs compiling first)
BAT – executable batch file (file of DOS commands)
COM – executable command file (machine language), type in the
      filename and press the Return key
DAT – data file (listable via the TYPE command)
DBF – dBASEIII, III PLUS, or IV file
DEF – program definition or setup file
DOC – documentation file, similar to DAT
EXE – executable file, similar to COM file, but must be allocated
      to a specific memory location
MSG – message file, similar to DAT or DOC
OVL – overlay file (used by large programs)
PRN – printer file (can be modified prior to printing)
SYS – operating system file (like a device driver)
TXT – text file, similar to DAT, DOC, and MSG
WKS – Lotus 1-2-3 worksheet file
```

The $$$ extension is normally used by various application programs to identify temporary work files that the program intends to delete prior to completion. If you see any of these files on a directory listing, it is an indication that a program terminated abnormally, which could be due to a power failure or a user-initiated break.

## Wildcard Characters

**Wildcard characters** have been appropriately named because, like jokers in a card game, they can be used to represent different characters in DOS commands. The two wildcard characters used by DOS are the asterisk (*), representing a group of characters, and the question mark (?), representing only a single character.

Perhaps the best way to understand the use of wildcard characters is by example. If you wished to display a directory listing of all the files on Drive A that begin with the characters LTR and that have an extension of DOC, you could enter the following directory command: **DIR A:LTR\*.DOC**. In this example, the asterisk substitutes for any group of characters, so that filenames LTRSMITH.DOC, LTR4.DOC, and LTRBILL3.DOC would all qualify to be displayed in the directory.

If you wished to display all the files on Drive A that only contain a single character following LTR and contain any filename extension, you could enter: **DIR A:LTR?.\***. In this example, the filenames LTR1.DOC, LTR2, and LTRX.TXT would be displayed in the directory.

Wildcard characters can also be used with optional filename extensions. For example:

DIR A:TEXT.\*    (list all files on Drive A with a filename of TEXT)
DIR B:P\*.T\*    (list any filename on Drive B starting with P having an extension starting with T)

If you would like to try some examples using your DOS disk, enter the following three commands at the A> system prompt:

DIR            (list all files on Drive A)
DIR A:\*.EXE   (list just those files with an EXE extension)
DIR A:S\*.\*   (list just those files that begin with an S)

Figure 2-4 shows you what the display screen should look like after executing the last two commands, assuming Drive A contains PC-DOS Version 3.1.

**Figure 2-4**

*Screen Display of*
*Using Wildcards*

```
A>DIR A:*.EXE

  Volume in drive A is DOS DISK
  Directory of  A:\

ATTRIB   EXE    15091    3-07-85    1:43p
FIND     EXE     6403    3-07-85    1:43p
JOIN     EXE    15971    3-07-85    1:43p
SHARE    EXE     8304    3-07-85    1:43p
SORT     EXE     1664    3-07-85    1:43p
SUBST    EXE    16611    3-07-85    1:43p
         6 File(s)    44032 bytes free

A>DIR A:*.*

  Volume in drive A is DOS DISK
  Directory of  A:\

SELECT   COM     2084    3-07-85    1:43p
SHARE    EXE     8304    3-07-85    1:43p
SORT     EXE     1664    3-07-85    1:43p
SUBST    EXE    16611    3-07-85    1:43p
SYS      COM     3727    3-07-85    1:43p
         5 File(s)    44032 bytes free
```

# The DOS Directory Listing

When you get a **directory listing** on your screen, it displays more than just the filenames. The file size in bytes as well as a "date stamp" is also displayed for each file. The date stamp is the date and time that each file was last written to the disk. As the number of files saved becomes large, the correct date stamp becomes even more important. This is why it is important to enter the date and time correctly each time DOS is booted. Figure 2-5 on the next page shows you a directory listing of a sample DOS disk.

**Figure 2-5**

*PC-DOS Disk
Directory*

| Volume in drive A has no label | | | | |
|---|---|---|---|---|
| Directory of  A:\ | | | | |
| COMMAND | COM | 23210 | 3-07-85 | 1:43p |
| ANSI | SYS | 1651 | 3-07-85 | 1:43p |
| ASSIGN | COM | 1509 | 3-07-85 | 1:43p |
| ATTRIB | EXE | 15091 | 3-07-85 | 1:43p |
| BACKUP | COM | 5577 | 3-07-85 | 1:43p |
| BASIC | COM | 17792 | 3-07-85 | 1:43p |
| BASICA | COM | 27520 | 3-07-85 | 1:43p |
| CHKDSK | COM | 9435 | 3-07-85 | 1:43p |
| COMP | COM | 3664 | 3-07-85 | 1:43p |
| DISKCOMP | COM | 4073 | 3-07-85 | 1:43p |
| DISKCOPY | COM | 4329 | 3-07-85 | 1:43p |
| EDLIN | COM | 7261 | 3-07-85 | 1:43p |
| FDISK | COM | 8173 | 3-07-85 | 1:43p |
| FIND | EXE | 6403 | 3-07-85 | 1:43p |
| FORMAT | COM | 9398 | 3-07-85 | 1:43p |
| GRAFTABL | COM | 1169 | 3-07-85 | 1:43p |
| GRAPHICS | COM | 3111 | 3-07-85 | 1:43p |
| JOIN | EXE | 15971 | 3-07-85 | 1:43p |
| LABEL | COM | 1826 | 3-07-85 | 1:43p |
| MODE | COM | 5295 | 3-07-85 | 1:43p |
| PRINT | COM | 8291 | 3-07-85 | 1:43p |
| RECOVER | COM | 4050 | 3-07-85 | 1:43p |
| RESTORE | COM | 5410 | 3-07-85 | 1:43p |
| SELECT | COM | 2084 | 3-07-85 | 1:43p |
| SHARE | EXE | 8304 | 3-07-85 | 1:43p |
| SORT | EXE | 1664 | 3-07-85 | 1:43p |
| SUBST | EXE | 16611 | 3-07-85 | 1:43p |
| TREE | COM | 2831 | 3-07-85 | 1:43p |
| VDISK | SYS | 3307 | 3-07-85 | 1:43p |
| 29 file(s) | | | 77,420 bytes free | |

The directory can be displayed in three general ways. One way is to list all the files with all the information, one after another, until all files have been displayed. To produce this display, simply enter the **DIR** command at the system prompt. However, many times disks contain more files than can be displayed on the screen without scrolling. To get a directory listing of filenames one screen at a time, enter **DIR /P**. The /P option "pauses" when the screen is full and waits for you to press any key to continue. The slash (/) identifies a **command option** to DOS. The term "switch" is often used instead of a command option.

Another way the directory can be displayed is with the /W option. This option is helpful if you do not need to have the file size and date stamp displayed. It displays only the filenames, listing them five to a line in "wide" format. To use this option, enter **DIR /W**. Figure 2-6 shows you what the wide format might look like.

*Figure 2-6*

*Example of DIR with Wide (/W) Option*

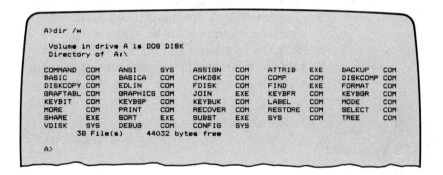

## Internal vs. External Commands

DOS commands are either internal or external. **Internal commands** are included with the portion of DOS that is loaded into RAM when the system is booted. They are available when the boot process loads the COMMAND.COM file from the system disk. Because it is much faster to access commands from RAM, the designers of DOS have made the more commonly used commands internal.

Some of the more commonly used internal commands include DIR, TYPE, COPY, and DEL. The DIR command was discussed previously. The TYPE command is used to display the contents of a "listable" file on the screen. It is often used to display the contents of batch files. The COPY command is used to copy a file from one location to another, optionally giving the duplicate file a new name. It is also used to copy characters from the keyboard (CONsole) to some device like the printer or a disk file. The DEL command allows you to delete unwanted files from a disk. These internal commands and others are discussed in detail in Chapter 3.

Because the full set of DOS commands is too extensive to be completely loaded into RAM, a substantial number of commands, called **external commands**, reside on the DOS disk. This could be either a floppy disk or a hard disk. External commands include all the filenames shown in Figure 2-5 except for the COMMAND.COM file, which contains the internal commands. Later on you will see how you can create your own "external" commands, referred to as batch files.

DOS automatically translates all commands to uppercase characters, so you may enter DOS commands using either uppercase or lowercase letters. Furthermore, commands can be entered using a combination of both types. For example, the commands Dir, dir, and DIR are treated the same way by DOS. To help you remember this option, our text examples use both uppercase and lowercase letters.

## DOS Versions

Figures in this chapter refer specifically to Version 3.x of PC-DOS, where x refers to any one of the modification levels. Major releases of DOS generally accompany a major change or improvement in hardware design. The first version, DOS 1.x, was somewhat limited and is now considered obsolete. DOS 2.x added hard disk capability, a necessity for most business applications. DOS 3.x added networking capability, better file management commands, and the ability to use the new 3 1/2-inch disks. Most colleges and universities use this version of DOS. The newest version, DOS 4.0, provides an easy-to-use file manager shell, direct support for hard disk exceeding 32 megabytes, and expanded memory support beyond 640KB. The DOS shell may prove a disadvantage to users because it occupies 256KB of RAM. By comparison, DOS 3.x occupies less than 40K.

If you have Version 2.x of DOS, it may be well worth a small fee and some restoring of files to upgrade to Version 3.3. The 3.x versions contain three useful additions:

**ATTRIB** — a command that allows you to protect a file by making it a read-only file (you cannot change a read-only file).

**LABEL** — a command that allows you to add, change, or delete a disk's volume label (its internal label).

**VDISK.SYS** — a device driver that enables you to use part of RAM as a very fast disk drive (called RAMDRIVE.SYS in MS-DOS).

# FORMATTING DISKS WITH DOS

☐

To save files on disk, the disk must be properly prepared to accept the data to be saved. When you purchase a new blank disk, it is a "generic" disk that can be used with many different microcomputers, including a variety of different operating systems. Therefore, each blank disk (floppy or hard disk) must be customized according to the requirements of DOS. This customizing process is called **formatting** and includes the operations described below.

(1) It creates addressable areas of the disk made up of clusters where data can be stored. Since each disk drive and operating system have their own addressing scheme, this activity is mandatory prior to saving files. With DOS 2.x and later versions, each of the 40 tracks on one side of a 5 1/4-inch floppy disk is divided into 9 sectors, for a total of 360 sectors. Each sector is designed to hold 512 bytes of data. A cluster is a corresponding track and sector on both sides of a disk.

(2) It then checks every recording spot on the new disk for damage and determines which clusters, if any, are not acceptable for storing data.

(3) Additionally, it creates a directory area and a File Allocation Table (FAT) on the disk that can be used by DOS to keep track of the files saved. The addresses of any unacceptable disk sectors and the addresses of all files saved are recorded in the FAT.

The **FORMAT** command is used to prepare a disk for use by DOS. When you format a disk, the system displays the status of your disk, including the number of any bad sectors it finds. Here is an example of the information displayed after the command FORMAT was entered and the disk being formatted had some unacceptable sectors:

```
362496 bytes total disk space
  8192 bytes in bad sectors
354304 bytes available on disk
```

A bad sector is a small portion of the disk that DOS determines is damaged. These sectors are noted on the disk's File Allocation Table. DOS does not allow data to be stored in these sectors. It is a good practice to replace disks containing a high percentage of bad sectors with good disks, as the cost of losing data is much higher than the cost of a new floppy disk.

The FORMAT command offers several helpful options. The system or /S option tells DOS to format the disk to include the DOS boot programs. When DOS formats a disk with the /S option, it actually writes three files on the disk. Two of these are hidden, which means you cannot see them when you display a directory of that disk. The third file is the COMMAND.COM file that contains all the internal DOS commands. To use the /S option, to create bootable disks, enter **FORMAT /S**.

Another helpful option of the FORMAT command is the /V option, which allows you to name your disk with a volume label. The volume label acts as an internal file label. This option is especially helpful when working with numerous disks, because it helps you keep track of your disks. Volume labels can be up to 11 characters long and you can create a different volume label for each disk. The label can be viewed on the screen without having to remove the disk from the drive, a requirement with external labels. To use the /V option, enter **FORMAT /V**. To use it with the system option, enter **FORMAT /S/V** or **FORMAT /V/S**.

Beginning with Version 3.2 of DOS, the FORMAT command no longer assumes you want to format the default drive if you enter the command without any parameters. This precaution keeps you from attempting to reformat your DOS disk accidentally.

# *Review Questions*

**2**

1. What are the main purposes of an operating system?
2. What is meant by the term "booting the system"?
3. What are the hidden files on a DOS disk?
4. Why is it advantageous to write on both sides of a floppy disk before moving to another track?
5. Why is it important to boot your system with the correct date and time?
6. What is the function of the File Allocation Table?
7. What is the difference between a warm boot and a cold boot?
8. How do you activate a warm boot?
9. What is the purpose of the COMMAND.COM file?
10. What is the purpose of the AUTOEXEC.BAT file?
11. How can you change the system date once the system is booted?
12. How would you enter a time of 2:35 p.m. when prompted to do so?
13. What does the command DIR B:/W do when executed?
14. What is the purpose of the FORMAT command?
15. What do the standard device names CON and PRN represent?
16. What is a filename extension and how is it identified by DOS?
17. What kind of file would likely have an extension of .$$$?
18. What are some common extensions for listable files?
19. What are some common extensions for executable files?
20. Why would you want to use the /S option with FORMAT?

# □ *D O S   Lab   Exercise   #1*

### *PLEASE NOTE:*

This exercise assumes that the system is already turned on from a prior class demonstration. If not, boot the system according to what you learned in this chapter. These exercises were developed for computers with two floppy disk drives. Drive A will hold DOS and Drive B will hold your working data disk.

If you are working with a hard disk system with only one floppy disk, the following modification must be made to your exercises:

The DOS commands should already be loaded on your hard disk (C:), so you should turn on the power to the CPU without having any disk in the floppy drive. Change any reference to Drive A in the exercises to drive C. Now floppy disk Drive A is used to hold your working data disk. Therefore, you must also change any reference to Drive B in the exercises to Drive A.

1. Warm boot:
   - With the DOS disk in Drive A, use **Ctrl-Alt-Del** to boot the system.
   - Enter the date in mm-dd-yy format (i.e., 9-15-90).
   - Enter the time in hh:mm format (i.e., 13:07).
   - Don't forget to press the Enter key (or Return) to cause the computer to act on your data.

2. Format a data disk to contain the DOS system files:
   - Enter FORMAT b:/s/v
   - Insert a blank disk in Drive B and press Enter.
   - Enter your name (up to 11 characters with no special characters) when prompted to do so by the system.
   - Enter n when prompted to format another disk.

Figure 2-7 shows you what the screen should look like when you finish formatting your blank disk.

**Figure 2-7**

*Screen Display of the FORMAT Command*

```
A>FORMAT B:/s/v
Insert new diskette for drive B:
and strike ENTER when ready

Formatting...Format complete
System transferred

Volume label (11 characters, ENTER for none)? Data Disk

   362496 bytes total disk space
    62464 bytes used by system
   300032 bytes available on disk

Format another (Y/N)?n
A>
```

3. Create a file from the keyboard:
   - Enter COPY CON B:READ.ME (or copy con b:read.me).
   - On the lines that follow, enter the following text, pressing the Enter key at the end of each line.

   *When entering DOS commands, the commands and parameters must be separated by delimiters. Delimiters are normally either a space, a comma, or a semicolon. They can be used interchangeably within any command (i.e., COPY A:oldfile,B:).*

   - When done entering lines of text, press function key **F6** (to tell DOS you are done with the copy operation) and press Enter. When pressed, the F-6 key displays a Ctrl-Z (^Z) on the monitor. The text you just keyed will be stored on the disk in Drive B with the filename of READ.ME.

Figure 2-8 shows you the screen after you have completed the COPY CON command.

**Figure 2-8**

*Screen Display of*
*COPY CON*

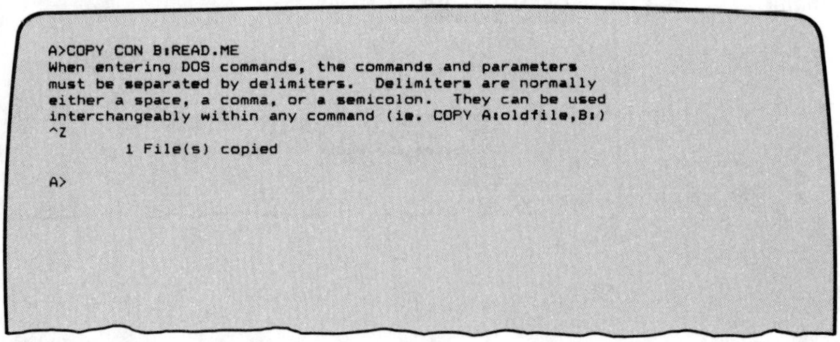

```
A>COPY CON B:READ.ME
When entering DOS commands, the commands and parameters
must be separated by delimiters.  Delimiters are normally
either a space, a comma, or a semicolon.  They can be used
interchangeably within any command (ie. COPY A:oldfile,B:)
^Z
        1 File(s) copied

A>
```

4. Display a disk file on the monitor:
   - Enter DIR B: (to verify that your file was stored). This listing should include READ.ME plus the COMMAND.COM file placed there during formatting.
   - Now enter TYPE B:READ.ME to see a display of your text file on the monitor.

   Figure 2-9 shows you what the screen should look like when you finish this portion of the exercise.

**Figure 2-9**

*Screen Display of*
*DIR and TYPE*

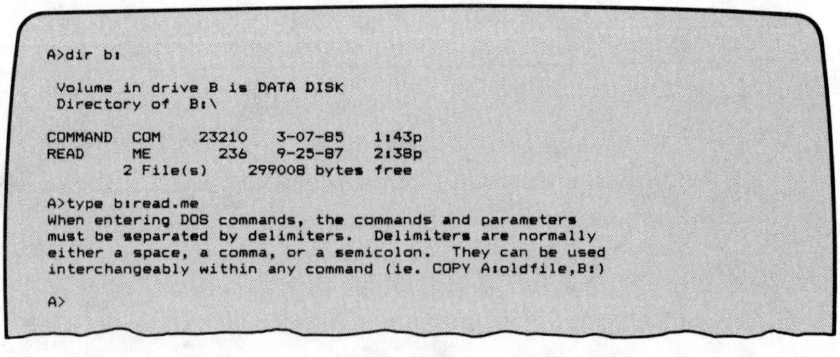

```
A>dir b:

 Volume in drive B is DATA DISK
 Directory of  B:\

COMMAND  COM    23210   3-07-85   1:43p
READ     ME       236   9-25-87   2:38p
        2 File(s)    299008 bytes free

A>type b:read.me
When entering DOS commands, the commands and parameters
must be separated by delimiters.  Delimiters are normally
either a space, a comma, or a semicolon.  They can be used
interchangeably within any command (ie. COPY A:oldfile,B:)

A>
```

5. COPY a file to a disk:
   - Enter COPY B:READ.ME B:READ.BAK. This creates a duplicate copy of your file, but with a different filename (the extension is .BAK rather than .ME).
   - Now enter DIR B: (to get a directory listing of B). You should have three files listed on your data disk: COMMAND.COM, READ.ME, and READ.BAK.

   Figure 2-10 shows the display screen at this point.

***Figure 2-10***

*Screen Display of
COPY and DIR*

```
A>copy b:read.me b:read.bak
        1 File(s) copied

A>dir b:

 Volume in drive B is DATA DISK
 Directory of  B:\

COMMAND  COM     23210    3-07-85   1:43p
READ     ME        236    9-25-87   2:38p
READ     BAK       236    9-25-87   2:38p
        3 File(s)    297984 bytes free

A>
```

6. DELete a file from a disk:
   - Enter DEL B:READ.BAK
   - Now enter DIR B: (to verify that the file was deleted).

   Your screen should contain data similar to that shown in Figure 2-11.

***Figure 2-11***

*Screen Display of
DEL and DIR*

```
A>del b:read.me

A>dir b:

 Volume in drive B is DATA DISK
 Directory of  B:\

COMMAND  COM     23210    3-07-85   1:43p
READ     ME        236    9-25-87   2:38p
        2 File(s)    299008 bytes free

A>
```

7. Change the default disk drive:
   - Enter B : (to switch default to Drive B).
   - Enter D I R (to get a directory of the default disk, Drive B).
   - Enter D I R  A : / W (to get a wide listing of Drive A).
   - Enter A : (to change the default drive back to Drive A).

Figure 2-12 shows the display screen when this exercise is over. Some of the data you may still have on your screen is shown in this figure. Don't be concerned if several of the top lines have scrolled off the top of your screen.

*Figure 2-12*

*Screen Display of DIR*

```
A>B:

B>dir

  Volume in drive B is DATA DISK
  Directory of  B:\

COMMAND   COM    23210   3-07-85   1:43p
READ      ME       236   9-25-87   2:38p
        2 File(s)     299008 bytes free

B>dir a:/w

  Volume in drive A is DOS DISK
  Directory of  A:\

COMMAND  COM    ANSI     SYS    ASSIGN   COM    ATTRIB   EXE    BACKUP   COM
BASIC    COM    BASICA   COM    CHKDSK   COM    COMP     COM    DISKCOMP COM
DISKCOPY COM    EDLIN    COM    FDISK    COM    FIND     EXE    FORMAT   COM
GRAFTABL COM    GRAPICS  COM    JOIN     EXE    KEYBFR   COM    KEYBGR   COM
KEYBIT   COM    KEYBSP   COM    KEYBUK   COM    LABEL    COM    MODE     COM
MORE     COM    PRINT    COM    RECOVER  COM    RESTORE  COM    SELECT   COM
SHARE    EXE    SORT     EXE    SUBST    EXE    SYS      COM    TREE     COM
VDISK    SYS    DEBUG    COM    CONFIG   SYS
        38 File(s)     44032 bytes free

B>A:

A>
```

8. Bonus exercise (requires application of prior learning):
   - If the system date is not the correct current date, use the **DATE** command to enter the current date. Otherwise, change the system date to yesterday's date. Use the **TIME** command to make sure that the system time is correct.
   - Use the COPY  CON command to create a new file called **B:EX2.TXT**. It should contain the following 5 lines of text, entered one line at a time. After entering the text, press function key **F6**.

*The Lotus 1-2-3 software package, as the name implies, has three logical and integrated parts: spreadsheets, graphics, and data management. Integration means that you do not have to leave the spreadsheet portion, for instance, to get to the graphing or data management portions.*

- Use the **TYPE** command to display this newly created file.
- Copy this file to a new file (on Drive B) with the same filename, but with an extension of **.DOC**. Use the **DIR** command to confirm the copy. The COPY command preserves the date stamp of the original file being copied.
- Notice what happens if you enter a command that uses wildcard characters incorrectly, such as DIR B:*X*.*. Modify this command to get a directory listing of all files on Drive B with an **X** in the second position of the filename.
- Using DOS wildcard characters, delete all files on Drive B with a filename of **EX2** and any extension. Before you enter this command, however, be sure it is correct, or you may delete more files than you intended. Two files should be deleted. Display a directory listing to check the status of files on Drive B. Does it look like Figure 2-11?

**This completes Lab Exercise #1. Don't forget to remove your floppy disks before you leave the computer.**

# INTERNAL FLOPPY DISK COMMANDS

## DOS INTERNAL COMMANDS

☐ BREAK (Control Break) Command
CLS (Clear Screen) Command
COPY Command
DATE Command
DEL (Delete) Command
DIR (Directory) Command
PROMPT Command
RENAME Command
TIME Command
TYPE Command
VER (Version) Command
VERIFY Command
VOL (Display Volume Label) Command

# 3

# INTERNAL FLOPPY
# DISK COMMANDS

*T*o make it easier to remember which of the commands are internal and which are external, the DOS commands covered in this chapter are all internal. External floppy disk commands are covered in Chapter 4.

This chapter covers 13 internal DOS commands likely to be used with floppy disk systems. Many of these commands are also applicable to hard disk systems, but do not necessarily require hard disks. More advanced DOS internal commands, those used primarily with hard disk systems, are covered in later chapters.

Our discussion of each command includes the following items:

- **The general format of the command.**
- **An explanation of the command parameters.**
- **Helpful options when using the command.**
- **Some examples of usage.**

In addition to the command name itself, DOS commands can contain various **parameters** to indicate the target of the command, as well as **options** to indicate how the command is to be executed. Options are often referred to as switches. Command parameters and options that apply primarily to hard disk systems are bypassed for now.

If the format of a command has a parameter or option enclosed in brackets, that part of the command is not always required. Do not include the brackets as part of the command when entering it. Command options are always preceded by a **slash** (/). We have intentionally omitted command options that are seldom used.

A **delimiter** is a special character used to define the end of a word or specific portion of DOS commands. Commands and associated parameters must be separated by a delimiter. DOS uses a variety of delimiters, including a space, a comma, a semicolon, an equals sign, and the Tab key. The examples in this text normally uses a space as a delimiter. As mentioned in Chapter 2, you can enter commands using any combination of uppercase or lowercase characters.

You can stop execution before normal completion in a variety of ways. You can abort DOS commands while they are running by entering **Ctrl-C** (or **Ctrl-Break**). When commands display a large amount of output on the screen, **Ctrl-S** temporarily suspends the display. Pressing any key continues the display process. When software instructions direct you to "Press any key," this normally refers to any alphabetic (A–Z) or numeric (0–9) key, or the space bar. It does not refer to any of the special or control keys.

A command you enter may be rejected by DOS, spurring an error message such as "**Bad Command or Filename**." You see this message if the command entered was not spelled correctly or if a filename entered was not on the disk specified. If this error message appears, simply retype the command correctly.

If you attempt to read a disk and no disk is in the designated drive or the drive latch is open, you get the following two-line error message, where x is the disk drive with the error:

**Disk error reading Drive x**
**Abort, Retry, Ignore?**

If you get this message, correct the problem and enter **R** to retry. You can also enter **A** to abort the command or **I** to ignore the error condition. However, do not change disks before responding with Abort, Retry, or Ignore.

The space between the read/write heads and the surface of the disks is incredibly small. Therefore, any movement of the disk drive when the disk is operating can be very destructive. When you attempt to access damaged data or read an unformatted disk, you see the following message displayed:

**General Failure reading Drive x**
**Abort, Retry, or Ignore?**

For a more complete description of commands and error messages, consult the DOS manual.

# DOS INTERNAL COMMANDS

☐

Internal commands are contained in the COMMAND.COM file that is loaded to main memory when DOS is booted. Therefore, you do not need to have the system disk in a disk drive when attempting to execute any internal command. The internal commands, covered alphabetically in this chapter, include:

1. **BREAK** — turns the system break mode on or off
2. **CLS** — clears the screen of all data
3. **COPY** — makes a copy of a disk file
4. **DATE** — displays and/or changes the system date
5. **DEL** — deletes a file from disk
6. **DIR** — displays filenames from a disk
7. **PROMPT** — changes the system prompt
8. **RENAME** — changes the name of an existing file
9. **TIME** — displays and/or changes the system time
10. **TYPE** — displays the contents of a listable disk file
11. **VER** — displays the version number of DOS
12. **VERIFY** — turns the verify mode on or off
13. **VOL** — displays a disk volume label

## BREAK (Control Break) Command

Format: BREAK [ON|OFF]

The **BREAK** command sets a switch in DOS that determines when the system should check for Ctrl-Break (or Ctrl-C) from the keyboard. With Break set off (the default setting), DOS only checks for Ctrl-Break during input/output operations to the keyboard, screen, or printer. To direct DOS to also check for Ctrl-Break during disk I/O operations, you must set Break on by executing the BREAK ON command. This option is useful when you run programs that are difficult to stop. If you enter BREAK with no parameters, the current status of Break is displayed on the screen. This command is often included in the CONFIG.SYS file (covered in Chapter 8).

*EXAMPLES OF USAGE:*

```
A> Break on
```
(directs DOS to "break out" of a program as soon as Ctrl-Break is pressed)
```
A> BREAK OFF
```
(directs DOS to only check for Ctrl-Break during input/output operations)
```
A> break
```
(displays the current status of Break)

## CLS (Clear Screen) Command

**Format:** CLS

The **CLS** command clears the monitor (display screen) to all blanks.

## COPY Command

**Format:** COPY [d:]filename[.ext] [d:][filename[.ext]][/V], where the first filename is the source file and the second filename (optional) is the target file (the new file being created).

The **COPY** command lets you make copies of disk files to a previously formatted disk. It facilitates making backup or working copies of files without destroying existing files. Any files on the target disk with the same name as the target file are replaced by the contents of the source file after the COPY command executes.

If you omit the disk device designator (d:), DOS substitutes the default device. If you omit the optional target filename, the system uses the same filename as the source file. Be sure to include appropriate filename extensions. To verify that sectors written on the target disk were recorded properly, you can use the /V option. This option slows down the copy process, but it may be worthwhile if you are experiencing disk problems. For example:

```
COPY A:MYFILE.TXT B:MYFILE.BAK /V
```

**Concatenation**, the combining of two or more files, can be performed with the COPY command. Use COPY with the plus ( + ) symbol between multiple source filenames to combine two or more source files into a single, new target file. For example:

```
COPY A:FILEA.DOC+A:FILEB.DOC B:NEWFILE.DOC
```

Files combined with the other commands may have two **end-of-file** (or **EOF**) marks, displayed as **Ctrl-Z**. To make the file more useful, you can edit the file with the DOS line editor (EDLIN is covered in Chapter 6), removing the middle EOF mark.

You can copy a group of files with a single command by using wildcard characters with the COPY command in filenames and filename extensions. For example, to copy all files on Drive A with an extension of .DOC to Drive B, enter:

```
COPY A:*.DOC B:
```

If you specify the source file as **CON** (for CONsole keyboard), the target file contains characters entered from the keyboard. Type characters as you would from a typewriter, pressing the Enter key at the end of each line. Lines are limited to 127 characters each. DOS uses the Ctrl-Z to mark the end of a text-only file. To stop recording characters and insert the Ctrl-Z character, press the F6 function key, <F6>, followed by the Enter key. For example:

```
COPY CON A:KBFILE.TXT   (followed by lines of text and <F6>)
```

COPY CON can easily be used to type a "quick and dirty" small file of text, but it is not appropriate for larger files. DOS provides EDLIN (see Chapter 6) for larger text files.

*EXAMPLES OF USAGE:*

```
A> COPY *.* B:
```
    (copies all files on the default disk, Drive A, to the disk in Drive B, without renaming files)

```
A> B:*.DOC
```
    (copies all files on Drive B with an extension of .DOC to the default disk)

```
A> Copy filea.doc b:filea.bak
```
    (copies FILEA.DOC on Drive A to Drive B, renaming it FILEA.BAK)

```
A> Copy con B:read.me
```
    (creates a file on Drive B named READ.ME consisting of data entered from console)

```
A> COPY A:FILE*.DOC B:
```
(copies all files on Drive A with a .DOC extension that begin with
FILE to Drive B)
```
A> copy a.txt+b.txt c.txt
```
(creates a new file, C.TXT, as a combination of A.TXT and B.TXT)
```
A> copy filea.doc B:/V
```
(copies FILEA.DOC on Drive A to Drive B and directs DOS to verify
the copy)
```
A> COPY FILEA.DOC PRN
```
(copies an ASCII file to the printer)
```
A> copy con prn
```
(lets you use the keyboard like a typewriter)

## DATE Command

Format: `DATE [mm-dd-yy]`

The **DATE** command allows you to change the system date. If you specify a
new date when you enter the command, it is changed immediately. If you omit
this optional parameter, the system displays the current date and prompts you to
enter a new date. Press the Enter key if you do not wish to change it. If you
enter an invalid date, you are prompted to reenter a correct date.

*EXAMPLES OF USAGE:*

```
A> DAT⁻ 3/4/90
```
(changes the system date to March 4, 1990)
```
A> date 03-04-90
```
(also changes the system date to March 4, 1990)
```
A> Date
```
(displays the current date and prompts you to change it)

## DEL (Delete) Command

Format: `DEL [d:]filename[.ext]`

The **DEL** command deletes the specified disk file. If the drive designator is not
specified, the default drive is assumed. You can use wildcard characters (* and ?)

in the filename and extension, but do so with caution, as multiple files can quickly be deleted with a single command. If you use *.* to specify the file, all files on the designated disk will be deleted. When you attempt to delete all files on a disk, the DEL command gives you some measure of protection against eliminating files by mistake. It pauses to ask you if you are sure. You are not allowed to delete read-only files without first changing the status with the ATTRIB command, which is discussed in Chapter 4. Also, you cannot delete DOS hidden files.

The term "delete" may be a little misleading, since files are not physically deleted from a disk file. The DEL command merely causes the file's entry on the disk directory to be flagged as removed, thereby allowing other data to be written over the "deleted" file. Technically, the command replaces the first character of the filename on the directory with an ASCII 229 character, which often displays as a question mark.

Since the **ERASE** command is identical to the DEL command, you may use either command. ERASE is treated as just another spelling of DEL.

*EXAMPLES OF USAGE:*

    A> DEL a:Memo.txt
       (deletes file MEMO.TXT from Drive A)
    A> DEL memo.txt
       (deletes file MEMO.TXT from the default drive)
    A> del *.txt
       (deletes all files on the default drive with a filename extension of .TXT)

# DIR (Directory) Command

Format: DIR [d:][filename[.ext]] [/P][/W]

The **DIR** command displays a directory, or listing, of the files on a specified disk. The information provided in the listing includes the volume identification, the name of each file, the size in bytes of each file, the date and time each file was last written to, and the amount of free space left on the disk. If you do not designate a disk drive, DOS uses the default drive. If you specify a filename, the directory is limited to only that name. Since the filename can contain wildcard characters, the directory can be limited to a specific group of files.

Subdirectory names (to be covered later) are also displayed on the directory and are clearly identified with <DIR> in the file size field. Entries for the hidden system files are never listed, even when present.

Use the **/P** option to cause the computer to pause during the display of the directory when the screen is full. It continues displaying again after you press any key to signal you are ready to continue. Figure 3-1 shows what the screen might look like using the pause option.

**Figure 3-1**

*Screen Display of DIR with Pause (/P) Option*

```
dir a:/p

    Volume in drive A is DOS DISK
    Directory of  A:\

COMMAND   COM   23210   3-07-85   1:43p
ANSI      SYS    1651   3-07-85   1:43p
ASSIGN    COM    1509   3-07-85   1:43p
ATTRIB    EXE   15091   3-07-85   1:43p
BACKUP    COM    5577   3-07-85   1:43p
BASIC     COM   17792   3-07-85   1:43p
BASICA    COM   27520   3-07-85   1:43p
CHKDSK    COM    9435   3-07-85   1:43p
COMP      COM    3664   3-07-85   1:43p
DISKCOMP  COM    4073   3-07-85   1:43p
DISKCOPY  COM    4329   3-07-85   1:43p
EDLIN     COM    7261   3-07-85   1:43p
FDISK     COM    8173   3-07-85   1:43p
FIND      EXE    6403   3-07-85   1:43p
FORMAT    COM    9398   3-07-85   1:43p
GRAFTABL  COM    1169   3-07-85   1:43p
GRAPHICS  COM    3111   3-07-85   1:43p
JOIN      EXE   15971   3-07-85   1:43p
KEYBFR    COM    2473   4-12-85   4:22p
KEYBGR    COM    2418   4-12-85   4:23p
KEYBIT    COM    2361   4-12-85   4:25p
KEYBSP    COM    2451   4-12-85   4:24p
KEYBUK    COM    2348   4-12-85   4:26p
Strike a key when ready . . .
```

Use the **/W** option to display the directory in wide format, in which only the filenames are displayed across the screen, five files on a line. You can use the /W option to save display time and space.

*EXAMPLES OF USAGE:*

A> Dir
    (displays a directory of all files on the default disk drive)
A> DIR B:
    (displays a directory of all files in Drive B)
A> dir a:dog*.*
    (displays directory of Drive A, of only those files with filenames that begin with DOG)
A> Dir b:/p
    (displays the Drive B directory, pausing whenever the screen fills up)
A> dir /w
    (displays filenames on the default drive in wide format)

```
A> DIR B:/W/P
```
(displays filenames on Drive B in wide format, pausing after each screen)

## PROMPT Command

**Format:** `PROMPT [TEXT]`, where text is a variable-length string of characters. Text may contain special strings in the form of $c, where c represents one of the following character codes:

**t** — **the system time**
**d** — **the system date**
**n** — **the default (current) drive**
**g** — **the > character**
**_** — **an underline (used to skip to a new line)**
**p** — **display the current directory (Chapter 7)**
**e** — **send an ESCape character (Chapter 8)**

The **PROMPT** command allows you to change the system prompt from the default (A>) to whatever you want to make it. Placing a PROMPT command in your AUTOEXEC.BAT file ensures that your customized prompt appears automatically each time you boot. If you enter PROMPT with no text, the system reverts back to the default prompt. For more information on PROMPT, consult the DOS manual. Figure 3-2 shows the effect on the screen of executing the four examples of the PROMPT command shown below.

*EXAMPLES OF USAGE:*

```
A> PROMPT Command?
```
(changes the system prompt from A> to Command?)
```
A> prompt DATE = $d
```
(changes system prompt to display DATE = followed by the system date)
```
A> prompt Hi Fred $_$n$g
```
(displays Hi Fred on the first system prompt line followed by A>)
```
A> PROMPT
```
(returns to the normal system prompt, A>)

*Figure 3-2*

*Screen Display of*
*Changing Prompts*

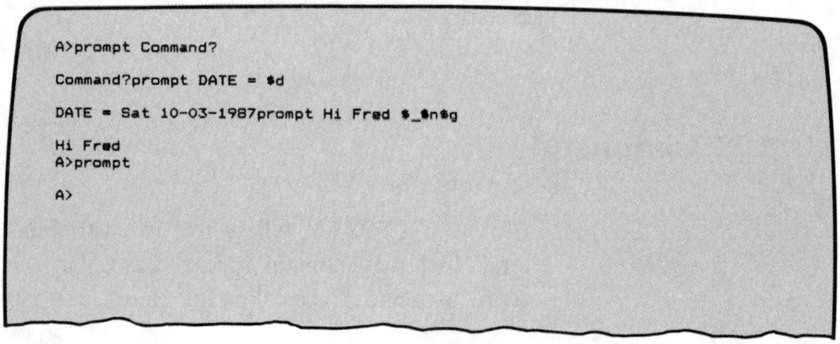

```
A>prompt Command?

Command?prompt DATE = $d

DATE = Sat 10-03-1987prompt Hi Fred $_$n$g

Hi Fred
A>prompt

A>
```

## RENAME Command

**Format:** RENAME [d:]filename[.ext] filename[.ext]

The **RENAME** command changes the name of the file specified in the first parameter to the filename and extension given in the second parameter. A drive designator is not allowed in the second parameter and is rejected if entered. RENAME gives you an easy way to make disguised copies of important files. For example, a spreadsheet file called BUDGET.WK1 could be renamed WORK.EXE. A shortened and commonly used version of the RENAME command is REN.

*EXAMPLES OF USAGE:*

A> RENAME b:ltr1.doc ltr1.bak
(renames LTR1.DOC on Drive B to LTR1.BAK)

A> ren Ltr1.doc Ltr1.bak
(renames LTR1.DOC on Drive A to LTR1.BAK)

A> Rename ltr1.doc *.bak
(renames LTR1.DOC on Drive A to LTR1.BAK — use of wildcard characters can save keystrokes)

A> REN *.TXT *.DOC
(renames all files with a .TXT extension to an extension of .DOC)

# TIME Command

Format: TIME [hh:mm[:ss]]

The **TIME** command allows you to change the system time. It is important to keep the correct date and time on the system because it is recorded in the directory information of each file you save. If you omit the optional parameters, the current system time is displayed and you are prompted to change it. To leave the time as is, just press the Enter key. If you enter an invalid time, the system prompts you to reenter a new time.

*EXAMPLES OF USAGE:*

> A> TIME 8:30
>> (changes the system time to 8:30 a.m.)
> A> Time 14:15:35
>> (changes the time to 2:15 p.m. and 35 seconds)
> A> time
>> (displays the current time and prompts you to enter a new time)
> A> time 11.55.30
>> (changes the time to 11:55 a.m. and 30 seconds)

# TYPE Command

Format: TYPE [d:]filename[.ext]

The **TYPE** command is used to display the contents of a "listable" file on the standard output device, normally the monitor. It does not alter files. This command should only be used for ASCII text files, not files that end with an extension of .EXE or .COM. Wildcard characters are not allowed. You can use TYPE in combination with the Print Screen capability of DOS to display the contents of a file on the printer. You can also redirect the output to a file or to a printer. Redirection of output is covered in the next chapter.

*EXAMPLES OF USAGE:*

> A> TYPE B:READ.ME
>> (displays the contents of READ.ME, stored on Drive B, on the monitor)
> A> TYPE read.me
>> (displays READ.ME, stored on the default drive, on the monitor)

```
A> TYPE AUTOEXEC.BAT >PRN
```
(The contents of AUTOEXEC.BAT are redirected to the printer)

## VER (Version) Command

**Format:** VER

The **VER** command displays the DOS version number being used on the screen (i.e., IBM Personal Computer DOS Version 3.10).

## VERIFY Command

**Format:** VERIFY [ON|OFF]

The **VERIFY** command sets the Verify mode in DOS. When the Verify mode is on, each character that is written to the disk is read to verify that it has been correctly recorded. With Verify set off (the default), DOS does not perform an additional read and compare operation each time data is written. To direct DOS to verify each write operation, you must set Verify on with the VERIFY command. Because of the extra time required to perform verification, it requires approximately twice the time to write data to a disk with Verify set on. Write verification is not recommended unless you are experiencing problems with your disks. If you enter VERIFY with no parameters, the current status of Verify is displayed on the screen.

*EXAMPLES OF USAGE:*

```
A> VERIFY on
```
(directs DOS to verify each disk write)
```
A> verify off
```
(sets the Verify mode off)
```
A> Verify
```
(displays the current status of the Verify mode)

## VOL (Display Volume Label) Command

**Format:** VOL [d:]

The **VOL** command is used to display the internal disk volume label of the designated drive, so you don't have to physically remove the disk from the drive to identify it. If you do not specify a drive, the default drive is assumed. The volume label can be created with the FORMAT command and later changed with the LABEL command. Both of these external commands are covered in the next chapter.

*EXAMPLES OF USAGE:*

A> vol B:
(displays the volume label recorded on the disk in Drive B)
A> VOL
(displays the volume label of Drive A)

# *Review Questions*

1. What is the function of brackets in this text for describing command formats?
2. What is the function of the slash in this text for describing command formats?
3. What is a delimiter and why is it required?
4. What does the message "Bad Command or File Name" mean?
5. Where are internal commands stored on a permanent basis?
6. When does DOS normally check for a Ctrl-Break (Ctrl-C) entered from the keyboard?
7. What DOS command blanks out the display screen?
8. What is the benefit of using wildcard characters in the COPY command?
9. What command lets you use the keyboard and printer as a typewriter?
10. What command removes the filename from the disk directory, but does not physically remove the file from the disk?
11. What option allows you to get a directory listing on the screen with filenames displayed in multiple columns?
12. What method is used to get a directory listing of a specific group of files?

13. What command is used to change the system prompt to display the system time?
14. How would you cause the system to display a customized system prompt every time the system is booted?
15. What happens if you include a disk drive designator on both parameters of the RENAME command?
16. What do you have to enter to change the system time to 4 p.m.?
17. What type of file is considered listable with TYPE?
18. What command is used to verify the DOS version being used?
19. What command is used to verify that data written to disk is correct?
20. What command is used to display the internal label on a disk without getting a directory listing?

# ☐ *D O S   Lab   Exercise   #2*

1. Boot DOS (Drive A) and insert your data disk in Drive B. Then enter DIR B: to refresh your memory of the files on Drive B. You should see two files displayed that were previously created in Lab Exercise #1: COMMAND.COM and READ.ME.

2. Enter VERIFY to see whether or not DOS verifies each "write" with an automatic "verification read." The responding message should indicate that the Verify mode is set off. Test the effect by entering the following: COPY A:COMMAND.COM B:TEST.1 and making a note of how long it takes to copy (i.e., 4 seconds). Enter VERIFY ON to set on the Verify mode. Enter COPY A:COMMAND.COM B:TEST.2 and see if the copy with the verification takes a substantially longer time (i.e., 7 seconds). Then enter VERIFY OFF.

3. Enter DIR B: to get a current directory listing of your data disk. Enter RENAME B:TEST.2 TEST.3 to change the filename of TEST.2 on your data disk to TEST.3. Enter DIR B: to verify the name change. To simplify the commands in this step, you could have first changed the default disk to Drive B and then omitted all reference to Drive B (B:).

4. Enter VOL B: to see if your data disk has an internal volume label. If you did not use the /V option when you formatted the disk (or have not yet used the LABEL command), your data disk should not contain a volume label.

5. Enter VER to see what DOS version you have (i.e., Ver. 3.2).

6. Enter DATE and follow the system prompts to change the current system date. Then do the same for TIME. Typically, you only need to enter hh:mm (i.e., 13:45) for the time, ignoring seconds.

7. Create a combined file: COPY B:READ.ME+B:READ.ME B:TEST.4. This creates a new file (TEST.4 on Drive B) as the sum, or concatenation, of two files on Drive B (READ.ME and READ.ME). Enter DIR B: to see if the combined new file is twice the size of READ.ME. In addition, enter TYPE B:TEST.4 to verify that the text in READ.ME was duplicated correctly. Your display screen should now look something like Figure 3-3.

*Figure 3-3*

*Screen Display of*
*DIR and TYPE*

```
A>dir b:

   Volume in drive B is DATA DISK
   Directory of  B:\

COMMAND  COM     23210    3-07-85   1:43p
TEST     1       23210    3-07-85   1:43p
READ     ME        236    9-25-87   2:38p
TEST     3       23210    3-07-85   1:43p
TEST     4         473   10-03-87   2:18p
        5 File(s)    250880 bytes free

A>type b:test.4
When entering DOS commands, the commands and parameters
must be separated by delimiters.  Delimiters are normally
either a space, a comma, or a semicolon.  They can be used
interchangeably within any command (ie. COPY A:oldfile,B:)
When entering DOS commands, the commands and parameters
must be separated by delimiters.  Delimiters are normally
either a space, a comma, or a semicolon.  They can be used
interchangeably within any command (ie. COPY A:oldfile,B:)

A>
```

8. Bonus exercise (requires application of prior learning):
   - Use the **BREAK** command to check the status of the Ctrl-Break mode. Set Break off if it is already on. After it displays the status, clear the screen to blank with the **CLS** command.

- Use the **COPY** command to copy B:TEST.1 to B:TEST.BRK. While it is executing, try to abort the execution by entering a Ctrl-Break (or Ctrl-C) command. When Break is off the entire file is displayed before the Ctrl-Break is recognized by DOS.
- Set Break on and delete B:TEST.BRK. Rerun the **COPY** command and attempt to abort the execution as before. You must act quickly, but it can be done! If the Ctrl-Break was successful, get a directory listing of Drive B to verify that the file was not copied.
- Using the **RENAME** command, change all files on Drive B with a file-name of TEST (any extension) to NEWNAME. Use wildcard characters whenever possible. Use the **DIR** command to confirm the results.
- Now, copy all files on Drive B with a filename of NEWNAME to a file-name of TEST, without changing the filename extension. Display all the files on Drive B to confirm this operation. Finally, delete all files on Drive B with a filename of NEWNAME.

**This completes Lab Exercise #2. When you are done, be sure to remove your disks.**

# 4

# EXTERNAL FLOPPY DISK COMMANDS

## DOS EXTERNAL COMMANDS

☐ ATTRIB (Attribute) Command
CHKDSK (Check Disk) Command
COMP (Compare Files) Command
DISKCOMP Command
DISKCOPY Command
FIND Command
FORMAT Command
LABEL (Volume Label) Command
RECOVER Command
SYS (System) Command

# 4

# EXTERNAL FLOPPY DISK COMMANDS

## DOS EXTERNAL COMMANDS

☐

All external commands are preceded with an optional disk drive designator, which the computer needs in order to identify the drive containing the external commands. For example, if the default disk is Drive B and DOS is loaded in Drive A, then A:FORMAT B: would be required to execute the external command FORMAT and format the disk in Drive B. If the designator is omitted, the system assumes the external command will be found on the default drive. The ten external commands covered in this chapter include:

1. **ATTRIB** — sets the read-only status of a disk file
2. **CHKDSK** — provides a disk status report and fixes disks
3. **COMP** — compares the contents of two disk files
4. **DISKCOMP** — compares the contents of two disks
5. **DISKCOPY** — makes a duplicate copy of a disk
6. **FIND** — locates a file containing a set of characters
7. **FORMAT** — prepares a disk for recording DOS files
8. **LABEL** — creates, changes, or deletes a disk volume label
9. **RECOVER** — recovers a file with defective sectors
10. **SYS** — copies the hidden system files to a formatted disk

The ATTRIB and LABEL commands were added to DOS Version 3.0. They are not available in earlier versions.

## ATTRIB (Attribute) Command

**Format:** [d:]ATTRIB [+R|-R] [d:]filename[.ext]

The **ATTRIB** command allows you to set or reset the read-only file attribute. This is very useful for protecting files in a shared or networked environment where you do not want others accidentally destroying your files. If you have important files that you don't want destroyed by overwriting, you can add a degree of safety by marking them as read-only with ATTRIB. Enter + R to set the read-only status and –R to remove it. Files identified as read-only cannot be altered without resetting their status with the ATTRIB command. You may use wildcard characters with this command. If you enter ATTRIB without the optional set/reset parameter [ + R | –R], the system displays the current status of the files specified. You must use utility support programs to set and reset other file attributes, like hidden files.

*EXAMPLES OF USAGE:*

> A> ATTRIB +r b:filea.txt
> (sets FILEA.TXT on Drive B to read-only)
> A> attrib -r B:*.txt
> (sets all files on Drive B with a .TXT extension so they are not read-only)
> A> B:attrib +R read.me
> (sets READ.ME on the default drive to read-only, using the system disk in Drive B)
> A> ATTRIB B:READ.ME
> (displays the read-only status of READ.ME on Drive B)
> A> ATTRIB +R A:COMMAND.COM
> (protects your COMMAND.COM file from being changed accidentally or by a computer virus)

# CHKDSK (Check Disk) Command

**Format:** [d:]CHKDSK [d:][filename[.ext]] [/F][/V]

The **CHKDSK** command produces a disk status report for a specified disk and lists the memory status of the system. It can also be used to fix logical errors in the way data was written to disk. After checking the disk, CHKDSK displays any error messages, followed by a status report. Refer to your DOS manual for a description of any error messages that appear. The following is an example of a CHKDSK status report, where the drive designated was a floppy disk and there were no errors detected:

```
Volume DATADISK Created JUL 15, 1990 11:35

    362496 bytes total disk space
     23528 bytes in 3 hidden files
    311296 bytes in 29 user files
     27672 bytes available on disk

    655360 bytes total memory
    568112 bytes free
```

The three hidden files in the status report represent the volume label and the PC-DOS system files (IBMBIO.COM and IBMDOS.COM) that are hidden from normal directory lists. The bottom portion of the report represents the memory status of a computer with 640KB of RAM. RAM is the computer's internal memory used to temporarily store programs and data during processing. The difference between the 655,360 bytes of total memory shown above and the 568,112 bytes free is about 85KB. That is the amount of RAM space allocated to the resident portion of DOS, including the space required to load and execute the CHKDSK command.

As we discussed in Chapter 2, new files are written to contiguous clusters whenever the first unallocated space found is big enough. The recording of an existing file that has been enlarged can cause problems, however. When the original file space has been rewritten, DOS continues writing to the next unallocated cluster on the disk. It writes in available clusters, skipping over those that are already allocated. Consequently, files can easily become fragmented as they expand over time.

If you specify a filename or filenames, CHKDSK displays the number of noncontiguous areas occupied by the file(s). Wildcard characters can be used for the filename. Thus, you can use *.* to determine the extent of file fragmentation on a disk and then use the COPY command to rewrite fragmented files to a newly formatted disk. This process is recommended to improve access speed.

**Lost allocation clusters** are parts of files that are still recorded in the File Allocation Table (FAT), even though they have been deleted from the directory. This logical discrepancy occurs because of some malfunction, often during the file save process. The usual causes of this damage are loss of power, resetting the computer during a disk write, a program going berserk, or just by hitting Ctrl-Break at the wrong time.

You can use the **/F** option to combine any lost clusters on a disk into a file named FILEnnn.CHK, where nnn is a consecutive number beginning with 001. This is a good command to use periodically, especially if a disk has experienced numerous problems. When the FAT is corrupted, it cannot accurately track files on disk. Therefore, the /F option could result in some loss of data during the fix process. When you use CHKDSK without the /F option and errors are detected, you must run it a second time with the /F option to correct those errors.

The **/V** option allows you to display all files and their complete pathname (paths are covered in Chapter 7) from a specified drive. This option can be very beneficial with hard disk systems.

*EXAMPLES OF USAGE:*

    A> CHKDSK
    (displays a status report for the default drive)
    A> chkdsk /f
    (displays a status report for Drive A and fixes any errors found in the
    FAT)
    A> b:chkdsk a:*.*
    (displays a status report for Drive A and lists any fragmented files)
    A> chkdsk B:read.me
    (displays a status report for Drive B and displays the number of non-
    contiguous areas contained in READ.ME)

# COMP (Compare Files) Command

    Format: [d:]COMP [d:][filename[.ext]] [d:][filename
            [.ext]]

The **COMP** command compares the contents of the first file specified to the contents of the second file. You can use this command to compare two supposedly identical files. When the files are not the same, DOS displays an error message for each location that does not match. After ten mismatches, DOS cancels the operation. Obviously, files must be of the same length to be compared. Wildcard characters can be used, allowing multiple sets of files to be compared. If you do not include any filenames, the system prompts you to enter them.

*EXAMPLES OF USAGE:*

A> B:COMP
(executes the COMP command from Drive B, directing the system to prompt you for the files — this method of execution gives you time to replace the system disk with another disk, if required)
A> comp filea.doc filea.bak
(compares the two files specified to see if they are identical)
A> Comp A:*.* b:
(compares all identically named files on the two drives specified)

# DISKCOMP Command

**Format:** [d:]DISKCOMP [d:[d:]]

The **DISKCOMP** command compares the contents of the two drives specified. It is only used to compare two entire floppy disks, but not hard disks. It could be a good command to use if you were making numerous copies of a disk and wanted to verify that they were all identical.

*EXAMPLES OF USAGE:*

A> diskcomp a: b:
(compares the disk in Drive A with the one in Drive B)
A> DISKCOMP A:
(compares one disk in Drive A with another to be placed in Drive A later; required in single floppy disk systems)

# DISKCOPY Command

**Format:** [d:]DISKCOPY [d:[d:]]

The **DISKCOPY** command copies the entire contents of one floppy disk to another. It does not require that the target disk be formatted. For this reason, it is *not recommended* that you use this command. By copying from one disk to another, it is possible that any bad sectors on the target disk (those normally bypassed by using COPY or XCOPY) are overwritten during DISKCOPY. If you execute DISKCOPY, you should also execute DISKCOMP to verify that the disks are identical. Another potential problem can occur when DISKCOPY is used. Any fragmented files on the source disk are copied exactly to the target disk without correcting the fragmentation.

*EXAMPLES OF USAGE:*

A> DISKCOPY A: B:
   (makes an exact copy of the disk in Drive A onto a disk in Drive B; the target disk does not need to be previously formatted)
A> diskcopy a:
   (makes an exact copy of the first disk inserted onto a second disk to be inserted into Drive A)

# FIND Command

**Format:** [d:]FIND "text" [d:]filename[.ext]

The **FIND** command searches files for a given string of characters. It displays on the monitor all lines from the specified file(s) that contain the desired string of characters. The text entered must be enclosed in a set of double quote marks. Wildcard characters are not allowed in this command, but you may enter as many files as you wish, separating each with a space.

This command has some options, such as counting the number of lines containing the text or displaying the relative line number of each matching line. For more information about these options, consult the DOS Manual.

*EXAMPLES OF USAGE:*

> A> FIND "Harvard" a:coll.doc b:filea.txt
> (displays all lines in the files specified that contain the word Harvard, but not HARVARD or harvard — *case sensitivity is critical*)
> A> FIND "*.*" B:DOS.DOC
> (displays all lines in B:DOS.DOC that contain the string of characters *.*)

# FORMAT Command

**Format:** [d:]FORMAT [d:] [/S][/V]

The **FORMAT** command prepares a disk in the designated drive to record data acceptable to DOS. It also examines the disk for defective sectors, making a note on the FAT of the sectors that are bad. If you wish to make the designated disk a bootable disk, use the /**S** option. It formats the disk and copies the three system files, IBMBIO.COM, IBMDOS.COM, and COMMAND.COM, from a PC-DOS disk. In MS-DOS, the three system files are named IO.SYS, MSDOS.SYS, and COMMAND.COM.

To uniquely identify each disk, use the /**V** option. This option gives the formatted disk an internal volume label, consisting of a maximum of 11 characters. You can later change a volume label with the LABEL command.

All disks must be formatted before they can be used by DOS. Whenever you format a disk, all previously recorded data is destroyed. For this reason, many organizations hide their format command so it can't be used accidentally. Later in this text you will see how this is accomplished.

FORMAT produces a status report indicating the following statistics for the formatted disk: total disk space, space marked as defective, space allocated to the system files (when /S is used), and amount of space left for your files.

*EXAMPLES OF USAGE:*

> A> FORMAT b:/s
> (formats the disk in Drive B so that it contains the system files, making it bootable)
> A> format /s/v
> (formats the disk in the default drive to include the system files and a volume label)
> B> a:Format
> (formats the disk in Drive B, the default disk)

## LABEL (Volume Label) Command

**Format:** [d:]LABEL [d:] [volume label]

The **LABEL** command allows you to create, change, or delete a volume label on a disk. It is a good idea to label your disks internally so you can identify them using the VOL command without having to physically remove the disk from a drive. If you do not specify a label, the system displays the current label, if any. It then prompts you to enter a label or to press the Enter key to delete an existing label.

*EXAMPLES OF USAGE:*

> A> Label b: Fred
> (creates a volume label of Fred on Drive B)
> A> LABEL
> (displays the current volume label on the default drive and prompts you to modify it)

## RECOVER Command

**Format:** [d:]RECOVER [d:]filename[.ext]
   –or–
   [d:]RECOVER d:

The **RECOVER** command lets you reconstruct files from a disk that has defective sectors. You can recover a file containing a bad sector, minus the data in the bad sector, by using the first format of RECOVER. In addition, you can recover all files on a disk if the directory has been damaged by using the second format of RECOVER. The second format of RECOVER *should only be used* if the directory of the disk has become unusable. Recovered files may need editing to return them to their original, corrected state.

Use of the RECOVER command with no filename causes DOS to read the disk and recreate the FAT and the directory. It generates unique filenames in the form of FILEnnn.REC, where nnn is a consecutive number beginning with 001. It is up to you to figure out the original filenames, however. You might try comparing file sizes from previous directory listings and using the TYPE command to display the contents of listable files.

*EXAMPLES OF USAGE:*

A> RECOVER b:pgm.bas
(recovers a file called PGM.BAS on Drive B)
A> recover b:
(recovers directory for disk on Drive B)


# SYS (System) Command

**Format:** [d:]SYS [d:]

The **SYS** command transfers the hidden system files from the first drive designated to the second drive designated. If you do not specify the first drive, DOS assumes the default drive. It does not transfer the COMMAND.COM file, however. You must transfer COMMAND.COM onto the disk with the COPY command.

The SYS command can be used to transfer a copy of your operating system files to a program disk designed to use DOS, but sold without it. In this case, space at the beginning of the disk already would have been allocated by the manufacturer via formatting with the /B option. The SYS command transfers your hidden system files to the allocated space. It will be a bootable disk after you copy COMMAND.COM to it.

With SYS, you do not have to reformat your hard disk when you upgrade from one version of DOS to a higher one. Just boot the new version from a floppy disk and then use SYS to transfer the new version's hidden files to the hard disk. Then copy the COMMAND.COM file and the rest of the new version commands to the hard disk. Make sure that no older versions of DOS remain on the hard disk, or you will get an "Incorrect Version" error message.

*EXAMPLES OF USAGE:*

A> SYS b:
(transfers your system files to the disk in Drive B)
A> sys
(transfers your system files to the disk in Drive A)

# *Review Questions*

1. What distinguishes external commands from internal commands?
2. What command is used to set a file to read-only status?
3. How can you view the read-only status of files on a disk?
4. What are the typical hidden files on a system disk?
5. How can you determine the amount of file fragmentation on a disk?
6. What command can be used to fix a corrupted FAT?
7. What command can be used to list just the filenames on a disk?
8. What is the purpose of the COMP command?
9. What command is used to see if two disks are identical?
10. What is the primary difference between using the COPY command as opposed to the DISKCOPY command?
11. What command is used to display the lines of a file called B:WORK.TXT containing the string of characters Rbt. Smith?
12. How do you make a disk bootable?
13. What is the purpose of a status report when formatting a disk?
14. Why would you want to use an internal volume label?
15. How can the internal volume label be changed?
16. When you reconstruct files from a disk with defective sectors, what must you typically do before you attempt to use them?
17. What happens when you use the RECOVER command without any parameters?
18. What files are transferred to an existing disk with the SYS command?
19. Why would you likely use the SYS command?
20. What would be contained in a file called FILE001.CHK?

# □ *D O S   Lab   Exercise   #3*

1. Boot DOS (Drive A) and insert your data disk into Drive B. Enter DIR B: to verify the contents of Drive B. To set a file to a read-only status, enter ATTRIB +R B:TEST.3. To verify that it was changed correctly, enter ATTRIB B:TEST.*. If done correctly, TEST.1 and TEST.4 will not indicate a read-only status and TEST.3 will be a read-only file. An R is displayed to the left of read-only filenames. Figure 4-1 shows you what the screen should look like at this point in the exercise.

***Figure 4-1***

*Screen Display of DIR and ATTRIB*

```
A>dir b:

  Volume in drive B is DATA DISK
  Directory of  B:\

COMMAND  COM     23210   3-07-85   1:43p
TEST     1       23210   3-07-85   1:43p
READ     ME        236   9-25-87   2:38p
TEST     3       23210   3-07-85   1:43p
TEST     4         473  10-03-87   2:18p
        5 File(s)    250880 bytes free

A>attrib +r b:test.3

A>attrib b:test.*
          B:\TEST.1
R         B:\TEST.3
          B:\TEST.4

A>
```

2. To see if the two files you created in exercise #2 are equal, enter: COMP B:TEST.1 B:TEST.3. If they indicate not being equal, you may have made a keying error. If you were comparing COM, EXE, or SYS files, you would get the following error message: "EOF mark not found".

3. To give a disk on Drive B a volume label, enter LABEL B: and follow the system prompts to enter a label of up to 11 characters (i.e., DATADISK). Enter VOL B: to verify the new volume label. Does your DOS disk have a volume label? Use the **VOL** command to check, but *don't try to write one* if the DOS disk you are using is not your own.

4. To display all the lines in a file that contain a given string of characters (i.e., "delimiter"), use the FIND command. Enter the DOS command FIND "delimiter" B:READ.ME. If you entered the text correctly in exercise #1, only one line of text should be displayed containing the string of characters "delimiter." Figure 4-2 shows you the results of executing FIND.

**Figure 4-2**

*Screen Display of FIND*

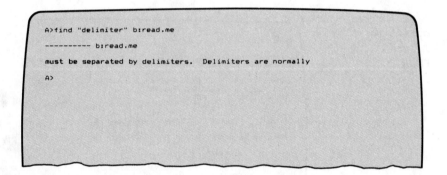

```
A>find "delimiter" b:read.me

---------- b:read.me
must be separated by delimiters.  Delimiters are normally
A>
```

5. Enter CHKDSK to get a status report of the default drive (A:). Then enter CHKDSK B:*.* to get a status report of your data disk, directing the system to check for any fragmented files. Figure 4-3 shows you the display screen after running CHKDSK. Your display screen should look similar to this one. Hopefully none of your files have noncontiguous clusters (blocks).

**Figure 4-3**

*Screen Display of CHKDSK*

```
A>chkdsk b:*.*
Volume DATADISK    created Jan 4, 1980 12:05a

    362496 bytes total disk space
     38912 bytes in 3 hidden files
     72704 bytes in 5 user files
    250880 bytes available on disk

    655360 bytes total memory
    609232 bytes free

B:\TEST.1
    Contains 2 non-contiguous blocks.

A>
```

6. Change the current DOS prompt to display an added message and the system date. Enter PROMPT It is $d$g What is your command? Execute a few commands (such as DIR, VOL, and VER) to see the effect of the new system prompt. Then return the system prompt back to normal by entering PROMPT $n$g. Figure 4-4 shows you the effect of experimenting with the PROMPT command.

**Figure 4-4**

*Screen Display of PROMPT*

```
A>PROMPT It is $d$g  What is your command?

It is Thu 10-01-1987>  What is your command?dir b:

 Volume in drive B is DATADISK
 Directory of  B:\

COMMAND  COM    23210    3-07-85    1:43p
TEST     1      23210    3-07-85    1:43p
READ     ME       236    9-25-87    2:38p
TEST     3      23210    3-07-85    1:43p
TEST     4        473   10-03-87    2:18p
        5 File(s)    250880 bytes free

It is Thu 10-01-1987>  What is your command?vol B:

 Volume in drive B is DATADISK

It is Thu 10-01-1987>  What is your command?ver

IBM Personal Computer DOS Version  3.10

It is Thu 10-01-1987>  What is your command?prompt $n$g

A>
```

7. Use **CHKDSK** with the **/V** option to get a listing of all the files on your DOS disk. Then use the same command to view the files on your data disk.

8. Bonus exercise (requires application of prior learning):
   - Copy B:TEST.1 to B:TEST.ROF. Set the new file to read-only status and try to delete it. Reset the read-only attribute (to allow writing to it) and then delete it.
   - Use the LABEL command to eliminate the volume label on your data disk. Use the VOL command to confirm that it is no longer there. Then change it back to its previous value. Use the DIR command to confirm the change. This exercise demonstrates that there are at least three commands that display a disk's volume label. Can you think of another DOS command that displays the label?
   - Use the FIND command to locate all the lines in B:READ.ME that contain the string "comma". There should be three lines. Then use FIND to locate all the lines that contain the string "a comma". Did you get the same number of lines? Why?
   - Change the system prompt to "What's next?". Use the CHKDSK command to get the status of Drive B, the status of RAM, and the amount of disk fragmentation on B:READ.ME. Notice the new system prompt? Finally, set the system prompt back to the default.

**This concludes Lab Exercise #3. When you are finished, remove your disks.**

# *Chapter*

# 5

# THREE IMPORTANT CONCEPTS

**BATCH FILES**
☐

**REDIRECTION**
☐

**PIPING (FILTERS)**
☐

# 5

# THREE IMPORTANT CONCEPTS

*T*his chapter introduces you to three different DOS concepts that can be very helpful. The first concept is the use of batch files, which allow you to automatically execute one or more DOS commands sequentially. Redirection is another important concept covered in this chapter. It is the technique used for changing the standard input or output device of a DOS command, thereby adding more flexibility to your commands. Closely related to redirection is piping (or the use of filters), a method of transferring the output of one command to the input of another, giving you a way to combine DOS commands.

## BATCH FILES

☐

**Batch files** are one of the most useful and powerful features of DOS. If you want the computer to perform a repeated, standard task or a set of DOS commands, you do not have to enter the commands every time you want to perform that task. With batch files, you don't have to duplicate your effort. When you create a batch file consisting of DOS commands, those commands can be sequentially executed by simply typing the batch file name. This concept works the same way as an external command. Whenever you enter the name of an external command, such as FORMAT or CHKDSK, DOS goes looking for it on the appropriate disk and executes it for you.

To give you a good idea of how batch file processing works, let's suppose you were tired of having to enter CHKDSK every time you wanted DOS to display a status report. You could create a simple batch file called **C.BAT** that would enable you to execute the CHKDSK command by entering **C**, your batch file name. You could use the COPY command to create a one-line batch file from the keyboard (CONsole) as shown below. It is very important to remember to press the Enter key after each line of instruction keyed. Pressing the F6 function key as the only entry of a line of text terminates the process of entering lines of text from the keyboard to a named disk file (in this case, C.BAT).

```
COPY  CON  C.BAT
CHKDSK
<F6>
```

Now, whenever you want to execute the CHKDSK command (for the default drive), you only need to enter the batch file command C to execute the batch file. This may not seem like a big deal, yet it reduces the number of keystrokes for the CHKDSK command considerably.

The most common batch file is **AUTOEXEC.BAT**, appropriately named for the term AUTOmatic EXECution. Immediately after DOS is booted, a ROM chip searches for an AUTOEXEC.BAT file on the system disk. If found, it will execute the predefined set of DOS commands contained in that file. Additionally, it will bypass the automatic prompting for DATE and TIME. You can add these commands to your AUTOEXEC.BAT file, or you can set the correct date and time from a battery-powered clock, assuming one is installed on your system.

Suppose you were setting up an office accounting system that required a specific set of tasks to be done whenever the system was booted. You could create an AUTOEXEC.BAT file containing the specific DOS commands you require. This batch file might look like this:

```
SETCLOCK
COPY  B:BUDGET.WKS  B:BUDGET.BAK
LOTUS
```

The computer would then execute these commands each time the system was turned on. This approach would greatly simplify and standardize the start-up procedures for your accounting system.

The first example of a batch file discussed was a simple one used to reduce the CHKDSK command to the letter C. But it was only able to execute CHKDSK for Drive A. What if you wanted to get a CHKDSK status report for Drive B? Since many DOS commands must work with variable parameters, a nifty batch file feature lets you substitute variable data into batch files. Batch files utilize a special symbol, %n, that allows variable data to be substituted in its place. You may often need more than one variable parameter in batch files, so a number (ranging from 1 to 9) follows the percent sign (%) to indicate which parameter is used. This gives you nine different values that can be substituted into your batch file.

The batch file above (C.BAT) could have been just as easily created with a single **replaceable parameter** (%1) that would allow you to designate a particular disk drive when you executed the batch file. You would need to change the command CHKDSK (in the batch file) to CHKDSK %1. Then, whenever the batch file is executed, the disk drive must be included as a parameter to be substituted for the %1 entry in the batch file. For example, you could enter C B: to display a CHKDSK status report for Drive B. The value B: would be substituted for %1 in the batch file during executing of the CHKDSK command. Likewise, C A: would cause the batch file to execute the CHKDSK command for Drive A.

The following sample batch file (called **COPYTXT.BAT**) allows you to make a backup copy of any .TXT file you chose and then obtain a directory listing to visually verify that the copy was completed. It contains two statements and three replaceable parameters as follows:

```
COPY  %2%1.TXT  %3%1.BAK
DIR  %3  /P
```

This batch file looks a lot more complicated than the previous example because it contains three replaceable parameters. Remember that the %n goes in the batch file when it is created and is replaced by the appropriate value when it is executed. The parameters to be replaced in this batch file are as follows:

%1 represents the filename to be copied.
%2 represents the disk drive of the original (source) file.
%3 represents the disk drive of the new (target) file.

A batch file is executed by entering the batch file name followed by the required parameters. Each parameter must be entered in the correct order. For example, if you wanted to use this batch file to make a backup copy of BUDGET.TXT on Drive A by copying it to Drive B with a new extension of .BAK, you could enter:

```
COPYTXT BUDGET A: B:
```

The three parameters supplied with the batch file name during execution of the batch file (BUDGET, A:, and B:) are substituted for the replaceable parameters (%1, %2, and %3) in the batch file. In effect, the execution of this batch file with these three parameters would be identical to entering the commands:

```
COPY  A:BUDGET.TXT  B:BUDGET.BAK
DIR  B: /P
```

Besides the normal DOS commands available for use in batch files, several additional commands improve the power and usefulness of batch file processing. In this chapter we introduce you to three useful batch file commands:

**REM** — Provides for remarks in batch files.
**PAUSE** — Pauses to allow operator input into a batch file.
**ECHO** — Sets the batch file echo feature on or off.

The **REM** (or **remark**) command allows you to document your batch files, making them more readable. These remarks can be displayed on the screen during execution, or shown only when the batch file is displayed with the TYPE command. Normally, we do not want to confuse operators with unnecessary messages on the screen. However, if you wanted to direct an inexperienced operator to insert a specific disk during the processing of a batch file, you could include the following command in the batch file:

REM  INSERT THE DATA DISK INTO DRIVE B AND PRESS ENTER

However, the operator would not have time to read the message, much less take the appropriate action, before the next batch file command was executed. Fortunately, DOS provides a method for pausing execution long enough to allow you to do something before continuing. The command used is named **PAUSE**. Whenever the PAUSE command executes, it halts execution until you signal it to continue. It automatically displays the message: "Strike a key when ready ." on the screen.

Another batch file command used to improve communication during execution is the **ECHO** command. It has several variations. If you put the command ECHO OFF in your batch file, DOS will not display (or echo) any of the batch file commands that follow it during execution. This situation can be reversed at any time. If you put ECHO ON in your batch file, all subsequent commands (including REMs) will be displayed on the screen during execution. If you use the ECHO command with a message after it, that message will be displayed, even if you had previously indicated ECHO OFF. An example of a batch file that uses several of these commands is provided in Figure 5-1.

***Figure 5-1***

*Sample Batch File*
*(L.BAT)*

```
ECHO OFF
REM  BATCH FILE NAMED L.BAT
ECHO PROCEDURE TO EXECUTE LOTUS 1-2-3
ECHO PLACE THE LOTUS DATA DISK IN DRIVE B
PAUSE
LOTUS
```

To execute the sample batch file in Figure 5-1, you would enter the batch file name (**L**) without the extension. When DOS executes the first command in the batch file, it sets the echo mode off, so the following REM command would not be displayed. The REM is included in the batch file for documentation purposes only and could be displayed whenever the TYPE command is used to view the batch file contents. In this example, the two ECHO messages would be displayed and the system would pause, waiting for any key to be pressed before continuing. It would then execute the last batch file command, the one that runs LOTUS 1-2-3. Figure 5-2 on the next page shows you what the screen displays would look like after executing the first five lines of the batch file.

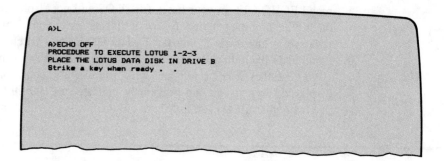

***Figure 5-2***

*Screen Messages*
*from the Batch*
*File*

Several fine points relating to batch files are worth mentioning:

1. If you begin a batch file statement with a *colon* (:), it will act as a remark that *only* prints when the file is displayed (with TYPE or EDLIN).
2. To issue a "beep" in a batch file (for alerting the operator to some action or problem), use ECHO <Ctrl-G>.
3. If you enter ECHO OFF at the system prompt, the system prompt will disappear until you enter ECHO ON again or reboot the system.
4. If you press Ctrl-C (Ctrl-Break) when a batch file is executing, you will be prompted with a message that asks you if you wish to terminate the batch job.
5. Other batch files can be executed from within a batch file. The last command of a batch file can even be another batch file.
6. Although the COPY command (with CON) can be used to create relatively simple batch files, it cannot be used for modifying existing batch files. For this you need a text editor like the DOS EDLIN command (covered in Chapter 6) or a word processor.

For a more detailed explanation of batch files and associated batch file commands, refer to the DOS Manual.

# REDIRECTION

☐

**Redirection** is the concept of reorienting the standard input or output device used by a command to another input or output device. The standard input device is the keyboard, while the standard output device is the display screen. The "less than" sign (<) establishes a new source of input and the "greater than" sign (>) establishes a new target of output. In the examples that follow, the first > symbol is part of the system prompt.

*EXAMPLES OF USAGE:*

    A> `DIR > B:DIR.LST`
        (redirects the output display of the DIR command from the screen to a file on Drive B named DIR.LST)

    A> `dir > prn`
        (directs the DIR display to go to the printer)

    A> `Sort < B:filea.txt > B:fileb.txt`
        (uses FILEA.TXT as the input for a SORT command that outputs the sorted results to FILEB.TXT — SORT is one of the filters, covered next)

# PIPING (FILTERS)

☐

**Piping** is a way of telling DOS to transfer the output from one command to become the input for another command. It accomplishes this transferal by creating a temporary file on the default disk for each "piped" set of data. The first command outputs to a temporary pipe file that is read by the second command. If piping requires many operations, multiple pipes are created. When the operation is completed, DOS deletes the temporary files. You can think of piping as a form of redirection. The major difference is that with piping, the temporary file is created by DOS and not by the user.

Piping usually involves the use of special commands, termed **filters**, that accept data, do something with it, and then pass it to the next step. DOS uses three standard filters in piping:

**FIND** — searches a file for a specified string of text.
**MORE** — displays only one screen of output at a time, waiting for the user
        to press any key to continue.
**SORT** — sorts disk records into a desired sequence.

The symbol used by DOS to indicate a piping operation is the broken vertical bar ( ¦ ). The standard output device for both the DIR and SORT command is the monitor. If you pipe the output from a DIR command into the SORT command, then the output displayed on the monitor will be the sorted listing of the directory in ascending sequence. For example:

```
DIR ¦ SORT
```

The above example is equivalent to the following set of commands:

```
DIR > A:TEMPFILE.$$$
A:TEMPFILE.$$$ < SORT
DEL A:TEMPFILE.$$$
```

To reverse the order of a sort, just tack on /R. The following command will produce a directory in descending order:

```
DIR ¦ SORT /R
```

If you find that the sorted directory is too large to fit on a single screen, you can pipe it to an additional command as follows:

```
DIR ¦ SORT ¦ MORE
```

Figure 5-3 shows you what the first page might look like when the above command is executed. The two strangely named files at the beginning of the directory are temporary files used by the piping process. DOS will automatically delete them at the end of the piping process.

***Figure 5-3***

*Screen Display of Piping*

```
        40 File(s)      41984 bytes free
     Directory of  A:\
     Volume in drive A is DOS DISK
     OC2E331E          0  10-04-87   12:46p
     OC2E3454          0  10-04-87   12:46p
     ANSI     SYS    1651  3-07-85   1:43p
     ASSIGN   COM    1509  3-07-85   1:43p
     ATTRIB   EXE   15091  3-07-85   1:43p
     BACKUP   COM    5577  3-07-85   1:43p
     BASIC    COM   17792  3-07-85   1:43p
     BASICA   COM   27520  3-07-85   1:43p
     CHKDSK   COM    9435  3-07-85   1:43p
     COMMAND  COM   23210  3-07-85   1:43p
     COMP     COM    3664  3-07-85   1:43p
     CONFIG   SYS      40  9-17-87   6:10p
     DEBUG    COM   15552  3-07-85   1:43p
     DISKCOMP COM    4073  3-07-85   1:43p
     DISKCOPY COM    4329  3-07-85   1:43p
     EDLIN    COM    7261  3-07-85   1:43p
     FDISK    COM    8173  3-07-85   1:43p
     FIND     EXE    6403  3-07-85   1:43p
     FORMAT   COM    9398  3-07-85   1:43p
     -- More --
```

If you want to display a directory of files that were created on a given date, you can use the piping concept as follows:

```
DIR | FIND "11-16-89"
```

Likewise, if you wanted a directory of files with an extension of .DOC, you could enter:

```
DIR | FIND "DOC"
```

In this example, FIND would not be able to locate any files if the search string was .DOC, because directory listings do not contain the period before the extension. In addition, it would not find any extensions of doc, because directory listings only contain uppercase filenames.

Piping and redirection can be combined in a single operation. If you wanted a sorted directory listing to be saved on a file called B:SORTED.DIR, you could enter the following:

```
DIR ¦ SORT > B:SORTED.DIR
```

Sometimes it is useful to display data from a listable file on the screen, but only one screen at a time. If ACCOUNT.TXT was a large file on Drive B that you wanted to display on the screen, you could enter:

```
MORE < B:ACCOUNT.TXT
```

This command directs MORE to get its input from B:ACCOUNT.TXT. Unless otherwise directed, MORE sends its output to the monitor one screen at a time.

The efficient use of batch files, redirection, and piping can be quite helpful. It provides you with a tremendous amount of flexibility to create your own customized commands.

# *Review Questions*

1. What is the purpose of batch files?
2. How are batch files identified by DOS?
3. What are two typical methods for creating batch files?
4. How are variable data (parameters) included in batch files?
5. When is an AUTOEXEC.BAT file executed?
6. Why are REM statements used in batch files?
7. When are REM statements in batch files displayed?
8. What is the function of a PAUSE statement in a batch file?
9. What happens when you enter ECHO OFF at the system prompt?
10. What is the standard input device in DOS?
11. What is the standard output device in DOS?
12. How would you use redirection to print a directory listing?
13. What kind of file is created with piping?
14. What is the purpose of the MORE filter?
15. What would be displayed by the command DIR ¦ FIND ".COM"?

# □ D O S Lab Exercise #4

1. For this exercise, you will be creating some temporary files on the DOS disk, so first you should remove any write-protect tab that is on the disk. Boot DOS (Drive A) and insert your data disk in Drive B. Then enter DIR B:. To experiment with redirection and piping, enter the following:

   DIR > B:TEST1.DIR
   (to redirect the directory from the monitor to a file named TEST1.DIR)

   SORT < B:TEST1.DIR > B:TEST2.DIR
   (to sort the previously created file and redirect it to another filename)

   DIR ¦ SORT
   (to list the sorted directory of the default disk)

   DIR B: ¦ SORT
   (to list a sorted directory of Drive B — the screen should look like Figure 5-4)

**Figure 5-4**

*Screen Display of DIR with SORT*

```
A>dir b: ¦ sort

        7 File(s)     246784 bytes free
   Directory of  B:\
   Volume in drive B is DATADISK
COMMAND  COM    23210   3-07-85    1:43p
READ     ME       236   9-25-87    2:38p
TEST     1      23210   3-07-85    1:43p
TEST     3      23210   3-07-85    1:43p
TEST     4        473  10-03-87    2:18p
TEST1    DIR     1657  10-04-87   12:50p
TEST2    DIR     1657  10-04-87   12:51p

A>
```

```
DIR ¦ SORT > B:TEST3.DIR
```
(to output sorted directory to a file)

```
TYPE B:TEST3.DIR ¦ MORE
```
(to display a file, one screen at a time)

Figure 5-5 shows you what the screen might look like after executing the last **TYPE** command and displaying the last screen.

---

**Figure 5-5**

*Screen Display of TYPE with MORE*

```
       40 File(s)      41984 bytes free
    Directory of  A:\
    Volume in drive A is DOS DISK
    OC361A4A          0  10-04-87  12:54p
    OC361C17          0  10-04-87  12:54p
    ANSI      SYS    1651   3-07-85   1:43p
    ASSIGN    COM    1509   3-07-85   1:43p
    ATTRIB    EXE   15091   3-07-85   1:43p
    BACKUP    COM    5577   3-07-85   1:43p
    BASIC     COM   17792   3-07-85   1:43p
    BASICA    COM   27520   3-07-85   1:43p
    CHKDSK    COM    9435   3-07-85   1:43p
    COMMAND   COM   23210   3-07-85   1:43p
    COMP      COM    3664   3-07-85   1:43p
    CONFIG    SYS      40   9-17-87   6:10p
    DEBUG     COM   15552   3-07-85   1:43p
    DISKCOMP  COM    4073   3-07-85   1:43p
    DISKCOPY  COM    4329   3-07-85   1:43p
    EDLIN     COM    7261   3-07-85   1:43p
    FDISK     COM    8173   3-07-85   1:43p
    FIND      EXE    6403   3-07-85   1:43p
    FORMAT    COM    9398   3-07-85   1:43p
    -- More --
```

2. If you are currently connected to a printer, you can complete this portion of the lab exercise. Otherwise, just read through it and use your imagination. To print a sorted directory listing on the printer rather than on the monitor, enter:

```
DIR ¦ SORT > PRN
```

To print a sorted directory of just those filenames on Drive B with a filename containing "test" on the printer, enter:

```
DIR B: ¦ FIND "TEST" ¦ SORT > PRN
```

3. Create a single command batch file that will automatically sort the directory of files on the default drive into alphabetical sequence before displaying it one screen at a time:

```
COPY  CON ASORT.BAT
DIR ¦ SORT ¦ MORE
<F6>
```

Enter the batch file name of ASORT to get a sorted directory of the default drive, one screen at a time. The output should look like what you displayed from the last command in part 1 of this exercise (Figure 5-5), except that this directory includes ASORT.BAT.

*Before you continue to the next exercise*, please remember to delete ASORT.BAT from the default drive (DEL ASORT.BAT).

4. Set up a batch file to prevent anyone from formatting a disk on Drive A by mistake. This batch file will only permit a FORMAT command to format a disk on Drive B. Enter:

```
RENAME  FORMAT.COM  FORMATB.COM

COPY  CON  FORMAT.BAT
FORMATB  B:
<F6>
```

Notice that the *original* FORMAT command had to be renamed so you could use FORMAT as the new batch file name. Then the batch file is used to execute the renamed format command (FORMATB) with the desired option, the formatting of Drive B only.

Remove the disk in Drive B and enter **FORMAT** to execute the *batch file* just created. When you get the message to insert a blank disk in Drive B, you can press Ctrl-Break to escape from completing the execution of this command. Figure 5-6 shows what the screen should look like after you terminate the batch file named FORMAT.BAT.

***Figure 5-6***

*Screen Display after Running FORMAT.BAT*

```
A>del asort.bat

A>rename format.com formatb.com

A>copy con format.bat
formatb b:
^Z
        1 File(s) copied

A>format

A>formatb b:
Insert new diskette for drive B:
and strike ENTER when ready^C

Terminate batch job (Y/N)? y
A>
```

*Before you continue to the next step*, delete FORMAT.BAT and then rename FORMATB.COM back to FORMAT.COM. Can you think of any other commands you would like to create?

*Before you begin exercise 5*, check your DOS disk to see if there is an AUTOEXEC.BAT file present. This can easily be accomplished with the command DIR AUTO*.*. If one exists, rename it AUTOEXEC.BAK. Then when you are finished with exercise 5 rename it back to AUTOEXEC.BAT.

5. Use `COPY CON AUTOEXEC.BAT` to create a batch file on your DOS disk containing the following commands:

```
REM SAMPLE INITIALIZATION PROCEDURE
ECHO  OFF
DATE
TIME
ECHO  ON
PAUSE  PLACE DATA DISK IN DRIVE B
DIR  A: > B:DISKA.DIR
DIR  B:
REM  END OF INITIALIZATION
ECHO  OFF
ECHO  HAVE A NICE DAY
PROMPT  DATE IS $D TIME IS $T $_WHAT NEXT?
```

Don't forget to press F6 and the Enter key to cause these commands to be written to the AUTOEXEC.BAT file. If you make an error after you pressed the Enter key on any line, you will have to cancel the process with Ctrl-Break and redo COPY CON from the beginning. When you are done, do a warm boot **(Ctrl-Alt-Del)** to boot DOS and have this new batch file automatically executed.

Experiment entering a few commands such as TIME, VER, and VOL with the new prompt. To change back to the original prompt, enter PROMPT.

*When you are finished*, copy AUTOEXEC.BAT to Drive B and then delete it from the DOS disk. If you previously removed the write-protect tab on the DOS disk, put it back on, covering the write-protect notch.

6. Bonus exercise (requires application of prior learning):

   ■ Enter: `SORT <B:READ.ME >B:READ.SRT` to create a new file, the sorted equivalent of the READ.ME file on Drive B. Use the TYPE command to display it on the screen. Notice that only the complete lines of text were sorted, not each word.

   ■ Enter: `TYPE B:READ.ME ¦ FIND "comma"` to display only those lines in the file containing the string "comma". If you are currently connected to a printer, you could redirect the output of this command to the printer by adding >PRN to the end of this command.

- Enter: DIR ¦ MORE. This causes one or two temporary files to be created by the MORE command, depending on the length of the directory listing. These filenames are created using randomly generated characters to avoid the probability of replacing any existing files. Use the **DIR** command a second time (without MORE) to confirm that DOS automatically deleted the temporary files after it was done using them.

**This is the end of Lab Exercise #4. Don't forget to remove your disks when you are done.**

# 6

# DOS EDITING CAPABILITIES

**EDLIN**
☐

**DOS EDITING KEYS**
☐

# 6

# DOS Editing Capabilities

*A*n effective operating system must provide the user with a relatively easy way to create and modify text files. In addition, it should have some facility for recalling previously entered keystrokes, thus saving the user from having to enter them again.

This chapter covers EDLIN, the DOS line editor. EDLIN is a mini word processor that lets you create and modify text files. This chapter also covers the use of the DOS editing keys. DOS editing keys let you quickly make changes to the last command entered, or to an EDLIN line of text, without having to reenter keystrokes.

## EDLIN

□

**EDLIN** is the DOS line editor that facilitates the creation and modification of batch files. EDLIN contains its own set of one-letter commands, which enable you to create and save files; update and edit existing files; and search, delete, or replace multiple lines or characters of text. You can use EDLIN as a rudimentary word processor. However, since EDLIN is line oriented, it is not recommended for the typical memo or document.

Line numbers are included for reference and are only displayed by EDLIN. Line numbers are never saved with the file. When you add or delete lines of text, the line numbers are *automatically updated* by EDLIN. If you refer to a line number greater than the highest line number in the text, EDLIN substitutes the highest number for the one referenced. The asterisk denotes the **current line**, which helps you keep track of where you are in an EDLIN file.

The format of the DOS command to execute EDLIN is as follows:

```
[d:]EDLIN [d:]filename[.ext]
```

If the file specified does not exist, EDLIN assumes you want to create a new file and displays "New file." At this point, you can enter **I** (for **Insert**) to begin entering text a line at a time. If the file specified is found, EDLIN displays "End of input file" and awaits your first command.

Although there are several other EDLIN commands, Figure 6-1 contains a summary of some of the most often used EDLIN commands with an accompanying explanation of each. These commands are entered at the EDLIN prompt, which is also an asterisk. This asterisk, the EDLIN command prompt, is displayed on the left side of the screen at position 1. The other asterisk, denoting the current line number, is displayed indented at position 11.

The general form of an EDLIN command is a line number (or range of numbers) followed immediately by an EDLIN command. In some cases, these single letter commands include optional parameters that must be separated with either a period or a comma. Commands may be entered using both uppercase and lowercase characters.

In the event that you are editing a very large file, refer to the DOS Manual for a description of the two applicable commands, Append Lines and Write Lines.

*Figure 6-1*

*Summary of EDLIN Commands*

**C (Copy Lines)** — Copies a range of lines to a specified line number and places them just prior to the specified line. For example, to copy lines 2 through 7 and place them before line 17, enter 2,7,17C.

**D (Delete Lines)** — Deletes a specified range of lines. For example, to delete lines 4 through 16, enter 4,16D. To delete line 4 only, enter 4D. Enter D to delete just the current line (the one denoted with the asterisk).

**E (End Edlin)** — Ends an edit session and saves the edited file. When you exit EDLIN, the original file (if any) is saved with a .BAK extension. The new modified file is saved with the name of the original file.

**I (Insert Lines)** — Inserts lines of text immediately before the specified line. When you create a new file, you must enter I before you begin entering text. To exit from the insert mode, enter <F6> or Ctrl-Break. For example, to begin inserting lines of text before line 15, enter 15I.

**L (List Lines)**— Displays lines of text from the file based on a specified range of lines. For example, to display lines 16–19, enter 16,19L. To display the 23 lines that surround the current line, enter L. To display a total of 23 lines starting with line 34, enter 34L.

**M (Move Lines)** — Moves a specified range of lines immediately before a specified line. For example, to move lines 14–27 immediately before line 4, enter 14,27,4M.

**Q (Quit Edlin)** — Quits the editing session *without* saving changes.

**R (Replace Text)** — Replaces all occurrences of a text string with another text string. For example, to change each occurrence of the word MS-DOS to PC-DOS in the first 25 lines of text, enter 1,25RMS-DOS<F6>PC-DOS, where <F6> is the F6 function key used to separate the two strings of text.

**S (Search Text)** — Searches the file beginning with a specified line to locate a specified text string. For example, to search the entire file for all occurrences of PC-DOS, enter 1SPC-DOS. The search command allows you to continue locating all occurrences of the specified string until the "Not found" message is displayed.

**# (line number)** — Directs EDLIN to display a given line number and lets you change it on the line below where it is displayed. This line number becomes the current line number. If you enter a new line of text, it will replace the old line as soon as you press the Enter key. You may also use the DOS editing keys to quickly make changes within the existing line of text. Characters to the right of the cursor when the Enter key is pressed are erased. Prior to pressing the Enter key, however, you can press Esc to cancel any changes to that line.

# DOS EDITING KEYS

☐

Frequently you will need to make minor modifications either to a line of text in a batch file (with EDLIN) or to the last DOS command entered. Rather than having to rekey the entire line of text or command, the **DOS editing keys** allow you to change only the characters that require modification.

Whenever you enter a line, DOS puts a copy of that line in a temporary storage location called an **input buffer**, so you can recall it and make modifications without duplicating keystrokes. The DOS editing keys are used to display the *last* line currently stored in the input buffer and to edit that line. The process of editing involves inserting and/or deleting characters in the line. You cannot just type over existing characters using the DOS editing keys. Figure 6-2 is a summary of the DOS editing keys that you should find most helpful.

*Figure 6-2*

*DOS Editing Keys*

**F1** — Display one character at a time from the buffer. (You can use the Right Arrow key to do the same thing.)

**F2** *x* — Display all characters in the buffer up to the given character (*x*).

**F3** — Display all characters in the buffer.

**Ins** — Insert one or more characters in the buffer at the cursor location.

**Del** — Delete one character at a time from the buffer.

**Esc** — Escape (cancel) the operation, leaving the input buffer unchanged.

Perhaps the best way to understand how to use the DOS editing keys is by example. The situations that follow demonstrate what you can do using the DOS editing keys. Practice these examples to reinforce what you have learned thus far.

1. Suppose you entered COPY A:TEST1.XT B:TEST1.BAK and got an error message because TEST1.XT was not found on Drive A (it should have been TEST1.TXT). To correct with the editing keys:

   ▪ Press **F2  X** (the F2 function key and the letter X) to move the cursor to the period just before the X, displaying COPY A:TEST1.

- Press **INS** and the letter **T**.
- Press **F3** to display the rest of the buffer. Now it should show `COPY A:TEST1.TXT B:TEST1.BAK`.
- Press **Enter** to execute the command and get back to the system prompt. It is okay to get an error message at this point since the file TEST1.TXT does not exist on Drive A.

2. Suppose you entered `COPY A:TEST3.DOC B:TEST.BAK` and wanted to redo it because you meant to copy to B:TEST3.BAK. To correct:

- Press **F3** to display all of the input buffer.
- Use the **Back Arrow** key to delete the last four characters (.BAK).
- Reenter `3.BAK` and press **Enter**.

3. Suppose you entered `TYPE B:TEST3.DOC` and got what you wanted, but now you also want to display B:TEST2.DOC.

- Press **F1** until the 3 in the filename is the next to be displayed.
- Press **DEL** to delete the 3.
- Press **INS** and **2** to replace the 3 that was deleted.
- Press **F3** to finish displaying the buffer and press **Enter**.

# *Review Questions*

1. What is the dual purpose of the asterisk (*) in EDLIN?
2. What does the EDLIN command 6,12D accomplish?
3. What happens when you exit EDLIN with the command E?
4. What does the command 1,1,8M do?
5. Why is EDLIN considered a very limited word processor?
6. What happens to EDLIN line numbers when lines are deleted?
7. What happens when you enter just a line number as an EDLIN command?
8. When can DOS editing keys be used?
9. What DOS editing key displays all the characters in the buffer?
10. How are characters deleted from the input buffer?

# ☐ D O S   Lab   Exercise   #5

1. *This exercise should be done in class as a group.* First, experiment with "beginning" EDLIN commands such as Insert, Delete, List, Quit, and End. For this part of the exercise, boot DOS, place your data disk in Drive B, and enter:

   ```
   EDLIN B:LINEDIT.DOC
   ```

   You are now ready to create a new text file. Enter the following commands (clarification comments are noted in parentheses):

   **I** (begin inserting lines of text)
   **ONE** (this is the first line of text)
   **TWO**
   **THREE**
   **.** (continue with FOUR through NINE)
   **TEN**
   **<F6>** (F6 function key and Enter to end inserting lines of text)
   **L** (list the lines of text entered)
   **4D** (delete line 4 of the text)
   **L** (list text again to verify deletion)
   **99I** (insert lines of text at the end)
   **ELEVEN** (this is the first line of text to be added)
   **TWELVE** (this is the last line of text)
   **<F6>** (stop inserting text)
   **L** (list text as it now stands)
   **4** (display line 4 and allow it to be changed)
   **FOUR** (change previous text in line 4 to FOUR)
   **L** (verify change)
   **5I** (insert text before line 5)
   **FIVE** (text to be inserted)
   **<F6>** (stop inserting text)
   **4,8L** (list only lines 4 through 8)
   **10,12D** (delete lines 10 through 12)
   **Q** (instruct EDLIN to quit without saving changes)
   **N** (abort the quit, useful if you entered Q by mistake)
   **E** (instruct EDLIN to exit and save the file)

2. Experiment with DOS editing keys by entering the following:

    `DIR A:`  (pressing Enter to execute this command)
    `DIR A:/P`  (using F3 to allow you to easily add /P)

    `COPY B:TEST3.DR B:TEST3.BAK`  (using no editing keys)
    `COPY B:TEST3.DIR B:TEST3.BAK`  (using the DOS editing keys to make corrections to previous entry)

    `EDLIN B:LINEDIT.DOC`  (recall previous text file)

**6I** (enter the insert mode)
**NOW IS THE TIME FOR ALL GOOD WOMEN TO LEARN TO USE COMPUTERS**.
**<F6>** (end inserting text)
**6** (list line 6 and allow for change)
**<F1> . . . <F1>** (press F1 29 times until just before the W in WOMEN is displayed)
**<DEL><DEL>** (press DEL twice to delete the WO in the buffer)
**<F3>** (display the remainder of the buffer)
**L** (list the file to verify the change)
**Q** (quit EDLIN)
**Y** (respond Y to verify the abort)

3. Experiment with "more advanced" EDLIN commands such as Copy, Move, Replace, Search, and Transfer. Enter the following:

    `EDLIN B:LINEDIT.DOC`  (to retrieve the file previously created)

**L** (list the file to refresh your memory)
**1,5,10C** (copy lines 1–5 before line 10)
**7,11,14C** (copy lines 7–11 before line 14)
**1L** (list lines of text beginning with line 1)
**1,19RTWO<F6>TO** (in lines 1–19, replace every occurrence of TWO with TO)
**1L** (list lines of text to verify change)
**9,19SFIVE** (in lines 9–19, search for and locate FIVE)

**18TB:READ.ME** (at line 18, transfer a file called READ.ME)

**1L** (list text)

**15I** (begin inserting before line 15)

**SIX** (line of text to be inserted)

**<F6>** (stop inserting)

**1L** (list text)

**16L** (list text beginning with line 16)

**18** (list line 18 and allow for changes to that line)

**<F1> <F1> <F1>** (press F1 three times to display the first three characters of line 18)

**TH** (add two more characters to that line)

**15L** (list lines of text beginning with line 15)

**E** (exit EDLIN and save changes to data disk)

4. Delete the AUTOEXEC.BAT file on Drive B that you created with COPY CON in Lab Exercise #4. Use EDLIN to recreate it.

5. For additional work, build a batch file on your data disk with EDLIN to create a new command for you. This batch file, called **MOVE.BAT**, will allow you to copy a file, give it another name, and then delete the original name. In other words, you will be creating a substitute for the RENAME command that allows it to rename a file and have the original file copied to another disk. The new batch file on Drive B should contain the following commands:

```
COPY %1 %2
DEL %1
```

This new batch file will be executed by entering the batch file name (B:MOVE) followed by two parameters (for %1 and %2). The parameter %1 represents the original filename and %2 represents the new filename. For example:

```
B:MOVE B:TEST3.DIR B:TEST5.DIR
```

Once executed, B:TEST3.DIR would be renamed B:TEST5.DIR. If you had desired, you could have easily specified that the new file was to be created on Drive A instead of Drive B.

6. Bonus exercise (requires application of prior learning):

Use EDLIN to create an AUTOEXEC.BAT file on Drive B to display a welcome message, request the system date and time, set the system prompt to display the current date followed by the > character, give a status report on available memory, pause until you press a key to continue, and clear the screen prior to displaying a directory listing of Drive B. This AUTOEXEC.BAT file should look something like this:

```
ECHO OFF
ECHO WELCOME TO DOS
DATE
TIME
PROMPT $D$G
CHKDSK
PAUSE
CLS
DIR B:/P
```

**This ends Lab Exercise #5. Remove your disks when you are done.**

# 7

# HARD DISK CONCEPTS AND COMMANDS

# 7

# HARD DISK CONCEPTS AND COMMANDS

Once you begin using a hard disk system, you will notice two significant improvements over floppy disk processing. First, the speed at which data can be transferred with hard disks is approximately 20 times that of the 5 1/4-inch floppy disks. The second improvement is the amount of data that can be stored on hard disks. A 20MB hard disk can hold the equivalent of about 55 floppy disks. These advantages can significantly change the way you use your computer.

The use of hard disks creates some considerations that are not necessarily relevant when using floppy disks. The first consideration is the need for a good power supply that does not permit loss of electrical power. A temporary power loss can cause the disk's read/write heads to "crash" on the surface of the disk, causing permanent damage. To ensure continuous power, a standby power supply (SPS) is often recommended for hard disk systems. The SPS, usually costing around $400, protects both the data stored on the disk as well as the hard disk itself.

Another consideration is the need for periodic backup of the data stored on your hard disk to floppy disks. Although this consideration is equally valid for data stored on floppy disks, hard disk users tend to overlook this process. Get into the habit of backing up your hard disks regularly. You will be glad you did the day you turn on your computer and hear a noise like a spoon in a blender.

One other consideration is the need to move the read/write heads to an unused area of the hard disk before you "power down" the system. When the power is turned off, the read/write heads on some hard disk drives do not retract automatically. Instead, they settle down on the surface of the hard disk. Over time, this process can damage data stored on the disk. If you have a hard disk that does not automatically retract the heads, you should execute a program like PARK or SHIPDISK that moves the heads to a vacant cylinder just prior to turning off the power.

# DIRECTORIES AND SUBDIRECTORIES

Because large amounts of data can be stored on a hard disk, it is extremely helpful to divide the total space into uniquely named areas. Each area can be reserved to store certain groups of files, thereby allowing you to organize and classify files by area. DOS uses a **root directory** and optional **subdirectories** (directories within a directory) to keep track of the name and location of all files on disk. You can establish subdirectories for floppy disks, but the use of subdirectories is generally more practical for hard disks.

One way to visualize the concept of subdirectories is to compare a single 20MB hard disk to a set of 55 floppy disks. Conceptually, each subdirectory could represent a single floppy disk, without the physical limitations of 360KB, however. And like floppy disks, each subdirectory could be devoted to a given application, like word processing, spreadsheets, accounting, and so on. Just as you change floppy disks, so you can change to another subdirectory. Additionally, just as commands like DEL, DIR, and COPY all relate to a given floppy disk, they apply to a given subdirectory.

With the release of DOS 2.x, you can organize and control hundreds of files on hard disk by adopting a tree-structured file directory system. The root directory branches into subdirectories. The subdirectories, in turn, can branch into further subdirectories in a hierarchy much like that of a family tree. Each subdirectory is assigned a unique name using the same rules we use with filenames. With floppy disks, files are often organized manually by recording selected groups of files on a disk and identifying each disk with a label. Subdirectories provide a big advantage in that they allow you to organize all the files on a hard disk "electronically." Within each directory, files can be added and new subdirectories can be created. Figure 7-1 shows a graphic example of a tree-structured directory.

**Figure 7-1**

*Sample Hierarchy of Subdirectories*

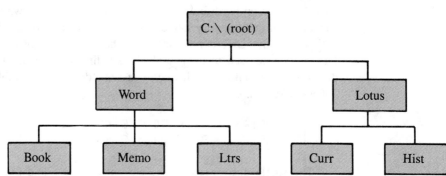

In the sample tree structure in Figure 7-1, the root directory is divided into two subdirectories: one for word processing and one for spreadsheets. The word processing subdirectory, WORD, is further subdivided into three subdirectories: one for a manuscript, one for memos, and one for letters. You can navigate through this structure by starting at the root and traveling down any of the desired branches to get to the desired subdirectory.

DOS uses the backslash (\) to identify a subdirectory name. Thus, the file BOSS.DOC stored on the MEMO subdirectory is identified with the full name C:\WORD\MEMO\BOSS.DOC. The full filename identifies a **path** of subdirectories that must be taken by DOS to find the file in the hierarchy. If the path is not included in the filename, the system looks for the file on the current directory. The backslash at the beginning of the path directs DOS to begin the path with the root directory. If it is not included, the path begins with the current directory. If the file you need is not on the current directory, you must provide DOS the path to find it. This path must be part of the full filename, just as the disk designator is supplied when a file is not on the default drive. Later in this chapter we discuss the PATH command. The PATH command is used as a default path for program files.

It is advantageous to set up subdirectories so that program files are separated from data files. This way, users can easily back up the subdirectories containing data files without having to back up the unchanged program files. Subdirectories containing program files only need to be backed up once, unless new programs are added.

DOS has a number of commands that allow you to create and use subdirectories. Any reference to the **"current directory"** refers to the subdirectory you are currently working in. You can change to another directory at any time. The root directory on hard disks can have up to 512 entries, where entries can be filenames or subdirectory names. Subdirectories are identified on a directory listing (via the DIR command) with the symbol < DIR >. The command DIR *. can be used to display all the subdirectories contained in the current directory. In subdirectory listings you see "dot" and "double-dot" directory entries, like this:

```
  .      <DIR>     8-15-90     9:45a
  . .    <DIR>     8-15-90     9:45a
```

The single dot represents the current directory and the double-dot entry represents the "parent" directory, one level up from the current directory. These two entries can be used as shorthand notation when referencing a directory. For example, the command "DEL ." is the same as "DEL *.*". To change to the LOTUS\HIST directory from the LOTUS\CURR directory, enter:

```
CD . .\HIST   (since both subdirectories have the same parent)
```

The following hints will assist you in correctly setting up the directory structure on a hard disk:

- Do not clutter up your root directory with lots of programs or data files. Generally, just a few files need to be in the root directory: hidden files, COMMAND.COM, AUTOEXEC.BAT, and CONFIG.SYS with its required device drivers (covered in the next chapter).
- Do not assign extensions to your subdirectory names.
- Do not nest your subdirectories more than 2 or 3 levels below the root directory.
- Give your subdirectories short but meaningful names like: \DOS, \UTIL, \WORD, \DB, \SS, and so on.

# HARD DISK COMMANDS

☐

Figure 7-2 lists and briefly defines eight of the commands you will most likely use with hard disk systems. Each command is explained in detail in this chapter, along with examples of usage. The commands are listed and discussed in a logical sequence rather than in alphabetical sequence to facilitate understanding.

*Figure 7-2*

*Hard Disk Command Summary*

> **FDISK** – Fixed Disk Setup, used to divide a fixed disk into one or more separate areas (partitions).
>
> **CD** – Change Directory, used to change to another subdirectory or the root directory.
>
> **MD** – Make Directory, used to create a subdirectory.
>
> **RD** – Remove Directory, used to eliminate a subdirectory.
>
> **PATH** – Instructs DOS where to look for command files.
>
> **TREE** – Displays the complete directory tree structure.
>
> **BACKUP** – Copies hard disk files to floppy disks.
>
> **RESTORE** – Restores hard disk files from floppy disks.

The format for all commands designated as external includes the optional parameter [d:][path] just before the command. These parameters may be used to designate the disk drive and/or the subdirectory path that contains the external command.

## FDISK Command (external)

**Format:** FDISK (requires the DOS disk in Drive A)

The **FDISK** command creates and manages partitions on a hard disk. Normally, you only have a single hard disk partition, devoted exclusively to DOS.

However, the capability exists to have multiple operating systems installed on a hard disk, in which only one can be active at any time. The FDISK command allows you to create partitions, change from one partition to another, or delete partitions. Even if you want just one partition, you must still run FDISK to allocate all of your hard disk to DOS.

When you first execute FDISK, choose the option that "Creates DOS partition." The system then asks you if you want to use the entire hard disk system for DOS. If you wish to have DOS as the only operating system, respond with a Y. Otherwise, respond with an N and consult the DOS Manual for further instructions. After the hard disk partition is established, you must run FORMAT to prepare it for recording data. Run FORMAT with the /S option to place the two DOS hidden system files on the disk. You should copy COMMAND.COM and all the DOS external commands to your hard disk and then put your floppy disk of DOS away for safekeeping. Once the system files are transferred to the hard disk, you can boot the system from the hard disk. When you turn on a computer with a bootable hard disk, do not have any disk in Drive A or the system will try to boot using the floppy disk.

## CD (Change Directory) Command (internal) — also CHDIR

Format: CD [d:][path]

The **CD** command lets you change from the current subdirectory to another one. The path is used to identify the directory you want to change to. For example, if you want to change to the root directory, you enter CD\. A leading backslash (\) in the path directs DOS to start the path at the root directory. Normally, you want to start at the root directory to make sure DOS is able to locate the appropriate subdirectory. You can enter the CD command with no parameters to display the current directory.

You can save keystrokes by recognizing that the symbols \ and .. are considered delimiters in DOS commands, just like a space and the slash (/). Thus, the command "CD\" is interpreted the same as "CD \". Likewise, the command "CD.." is the same as "CD ..".

The optional disk drive designator is used if the subdirectory you wish to change to is not on the default disk.

*EXAMPLES OF USAGE:*

    C> CD \
    (changes to the root directory)

    C> Cd
    (displays the current directory)

    C> cd\word\memo
    (changes to the subdirectory named MEMO on the WORD sub-directory, starting from the root directory)

    C> CD WORD\MEMO
    (changes to the subdirectory identified as MEMO on the WORD sub-directory, starting from the current directory)

    C> cd..
    (changes to the parent subdirectory)

# MD (Make Directory) Command (internal) — also MKDIR

**Format:** MD [d:]path

The **MD** command creates a subdirectory in a given location. You may create as many subdirectories as you want, but keep in mind that too many could cause confusion. Each subdirectory can contain both filenames and subdirectory names that can also occur on other subdirectories, but all names must be unique within a subdirectory.

*EXAMPLES OF USAGE:*

    C> MD\word
    (creates a subdirectory named WORD one level down from the root directory)

    C> md \word\MEMO
    (creates the subdirectory MEMO one level down from the subdirectory named WORD)

    C> Md games
    (creates a subdirectory called GAMES one level down from the current directory)

## RD (Remove Directory) Command (internal) — also RMDIR

Format: RD [d:]path

The **RD** command removes a subdirectory from disk. However, before you can remove a subdirectory, all files within that subdirectory must be deleted. In addition, all of its subdirectories must be removed. You cannot remove the current subdirectory without first changing to another subdirectory. You cannot remove the root directory.

*EXAMPLES OF USAGE:*

> C> rd \word\memo
> (removes the subdirectory named MEMO from the WORD sub-directory)
> C> RD\WORD
> (removes subdirectory WORD from the root directory)
> C> rd memo
> (removes subdirectory MEMO from the current directory)

## PATH (Set Search Directory) Command (internal)

Format: PATH [d:][path][;path][;path]

The **PATH** command allows you to direct the system to search one or more subdirectories for commands (or batch files) not found in the current sub-directory. With a tree-structured directory, you cannot always access any command just by entering the command name. You must specify the path by which DOS can locate the command if it resides on a subdirectory other than the current directory. The PATH command instructs DOS which subdirectories to search and in what order to find a command that is not on the current directory.

*PATH only locates files that can be executed.* Within each directory, DOS always looks for a matching command with a .COM extension first. If it does not find one, it searches for an .EXE extension, and finally a .BAT extension. Beginning with DOS 3.2, the APPEND command was added to allow users to set up a search path for data files. Consult your DOS manual for additional details.

A couple of other points concerning the PATH command should be mentioned. You are allowed to have only one search path active at a time. Typing PATH with no parameters displays the current path. Entering PATH with just a semicolon tells the system you do not want any search path. And finally, issuing a PATH command does not change the current directory.

*EXAMPLES OF USAGE:*

> C> `Path \DOS3`
>
> (directs the system to look on the subdirectory named DOS3 if it cannot find the desired command or batch filename on the current subdirectory)
>
> C> `PATH\word\ltrs`
>
> (directs the system to look on LTRS within WORD to locate a command if it is not on the current subdirectory)
>
> C> `path`
>
> (displays the current search path setting)
>
> C> `Path ;`
>
> (deletes any previous search path setting)
>
> C> `PATH \;\UTIL;\DOS`
>
> (directs DOS to search 3 directories in the order given: root, \UTIL, and \DOS)

# TREE Command (external)

**Format:** `[d:][path]TREE [d:][/F]`

The **TREE** command displays all the subdirectory paths on the specified drive. When the /F option is used, TREE optionally lists all the files in the root directory and each subdirectory. However, the TREE command does not create a very readable listing with the /F option. If you don't like TREE /F, try using CHKDSK /V. It lists all files, showing the complete pathname.

*EXAMPLES OF USAGE:*

C> TREE /F
(displays all the subdirectories and files in the root directory and each subdirectory)

C> tree >prn
(prints a listing of all the subdirectories)

C> CHKDSK /V ¦ FIND ".BAK" ¦ MORE
(locates every .BAK file in every subdirectory on Drive C, displaying them a screen at a time)

## BACKUP Command (external)

Format: [d:][path]BACKUP d:[path][filename[.ext]]d: [/S][/M], where the first disk drive designator after the command is the source drive and the second designator is the target.

The **BACKUP** command copies your hard disk files to as many formatted floppy disks as are needed to hold it in a compressed form. Beginning with DOS 3.3, the disks no longer have to be formatted before you execute the BACKUP command; it automatically formats new disks. You may include a filename to restrict the files you want to back up. Wildcard characters can be used in the filename and extension.

The BACKUP command provides you with several options that make it easier to control how you copy your files. You can use the /S option to copy subdirectory files, in addition to the files in the specified directory. The /M option can be used to back up only those files that have been modified since the last backup.

Whenever BACKUP fills a floppy disk, you will be prompted to insert a new diskette. Label each backup disk in consecutive order so you can restore them in the same order. It is important to remember that *BACKUP is not the same as COPY.* When files are recorded on the backup disks with BACKUP, they cannot be used until they are restored to the hard disk with the RESTORE command.

*EXAMPLES OF USAGE:*

> C> BACKUP C:\*.* A: /S
> (backs up all files in all subdirectories on Drive C to Drive A)
> C> backup c:\word\book\*.doc a: /m
> (backs up only files in the BOOK subdirectory within WORD that
> have an extension of .DOC and have been modified since the last
> backup on that subdirectory)
> C> Backup C:\*.txt a:/s
> (backs up all files on the hard disk with an extension of .TXT)

# RESTORE Command (external)

**Format:** [d:][path]RESTORE d: d:[path]filename[.ext]
[/S], where the first disk drive designator after the command is
the source drive and the second is the target drive.

The **RESTORE** command is used to restore one or more files from backup disks
created with the BACKUP command. When multiple backup disks are involved,
the system prompts you to insert the next diskette. You may use the wildcard
characters for filenames and extensions with the RESTORE command.

With the /S option, RESTORE automatically recreates deleted subdirectories on a hard disk, if needed. RESTORE can be used along with BACKUP to
transfer hard disk files to another hard disk. This feature could come in handy
if you wanted to store your files on a "loaner disk" while your disk is being
repaired.

*EXAMPLES OF USAGE:*

> C> RESTORE A: C:\LOTUS\*.*
> (restores all files on the LOTUS subdirectory from the backup disks
> on Drive A)
> C> restore a: c:\*.doc/s
> (restores from Drive A all files with an extension of .DOC for all
> subdirectories on Drive C)

# Review Questions

1. How are files arranged or organized on hard disks?
2. Why is a constant supply of good electrical power especially important when using hard disks?
3. What is the purpose of the PARK or SHIPDISK commands?
4. How are subdirectories designated in DOS?
5. What is a DOS path?
6. Why might you want to have relatively short subdirectory names?
7. What is the primary function of the FDISK command?
8. What command allows you to switch from the current subdirectory to another subdirectory?
9. How do you switch to the root directory?
10. How can identical filenames (i.e., FORMAT.COM) exist multiple times on the same disk?
11. What command creates a subdirectory named "DOS" from the root directory?
12. What command creates a subdirectory named "DOS" from the current directory?
13. What is necessary to be able to remove a subdirectory from a disk?
14. If multiple subdirectories are included in a search path, which one is searched first?
15. How are multiple subdirectories specified in the PATH command?
16. What command is used to view the current search path?
17. What command displays all subdirectory names on a disk?
18. What command is used to display all subdirectory names and their files on a disk?
19. What kinds of files can be recreated with the RESTORE command?
20. How can subdirectories be restored?

# ☐ *D O S Lab Exercise #6*

*These exercises do not require a hard disk system.*

1. Make a hierarchy of subdirectories on Drive B according to Figure 7-1 of this text as follows:

   ```
   A> MD B:\WORD
   A> MD B:\WORD\BOOK
   A> MD B:\WORD\MEMO
   A> MD B:\WORD\LTRS
   A> MD B:\LOTUS
   A> MD B:\LOTUS\CURR
   A> MD B:\LOTUS\HIST
   ```

   Did you remember to use the DOS editing keys to assist you?

2. Copy LINEDIT.DOC residing on the root directory of Drive B to each of the seven subdirectories created above.

   Example: `COPY B:LINEDIT.DOC B:\WORD`

3. Check out your new directory structure by entering:

   ```
   A> DIR B:
   ```
   (lists files and directories in root directory)
   ```
   A> DIR B:\word
   ```
   (lists all files and directories in \WORD — the screen should look similar to Figure 7-3 on the next page)
   ```
   A> TREE B:/F
   ```
   (lists all files and directories on Drive B — the screen should look similar to the last part of Figure 7-4 on the next page)

**Figure 7-3**

*Screen Display of*
*\WORD*
*Directory*

```
A>dir b:\word

 Volume in drive B is DATADISK
 Directory of  B:\WORD

.            <DIR>       10-04-87    2:23p
..           <DIR>       10-04-87    2:23p
BOOK         <DIR>       10-04-87    2:23p
LTRS         <DIR>       10-04-87    2:23p
LINEDIT  DOC     346     10-04-87    2:27p
MEMO         <DIR>       10-04-87    2:37p
        6 File(s)     229376 bytes free

A>
```

**Figure 7-4**

*Screen Displays of*
*TREE*

```
A>tree b:/f

DIRECTORY PATH LISTING FOR VOLUME DATADISK

Files:              COMMAND .COM
                    TEST    .1
                    READ    .ME
                    TEST    .3
                    TEST    .4
                    TEST1   .DIR
                    TEST2   .DIR
                    TEST3   .DIR
                    LINEDIT .DOC
                    AUTOEXEC.BAT


Path: \WORD

Sub-directories:  BOOK
                  LTRS
                  MEMO

Files:            LINEDIT .DOC
```

*(Continued)*

**Figure 7-4**

*(Continued)*

```
Path: \WORD\BOOK
Sub-directories:  None
Files:            LINEDIT .DOC


Path: \WORD\LTRS
Sub-directories:  None
Files:            LINEDIT .DOC


Path: \WORD\MEMO
Sub-directories:  None
Files:            None


Path: \LOTUS
Sub-directories:  CURR
                  HIST
```

```
Files:            LINEDIT .DOC


Path: \LOTUS\CURR
Sub-directories:  None
Files:            LINEDIT .DOC


Path: \LOTUS\HIST
Sub-directories:  None
Files:            LINEDIT .DOC


A>
```

4. Make the current directory MEMO:

```
A> B:
```
(changes default drive to B)
```
B> CD\WORD\MEMO
```
(makes MEMO the current directory)
```
B> DIR
```
(verifies change to desired directory)
```
B> CD\
```
(changes back to root directory)
```
B> DIR
```
(lists all files and subdirectories on the root directory of Drive B)

5. Delete the subdirectory named HIST:

```
B> DEL \LOTUS\HIST\*.*
```
(deletes all files from HIST first)
```
B> RD \LOTUS\HIST
```
(removes HIST subdirectory)
```
B> A:TREE B:
```
(tests the removal of HIST by running TREE — an external command on Drive A)

6. Set up a path to your DOS external commands:

```
B> PATH A:
```
(sets path to include Drive A)
```
B> TREE B:
```
(tests the path, noting that it will find TREE on Drive A after first searching Drive B)

7. Change the system prompt to display the current subdirectory. Then change to several subdirectories to see the effect:

```
B> PROMPT $P$G
B> CD\WORD
B> CD\LOTUS\CURR
B> CD\
```

8. Bonus exercise (requires application of prior learning):

- Make sure the default disk is Drive B. Copy at least three files from the root directory of Drive B to the WORD subdirectory created previously in this lab exercise.
- From the root directory of Drive B, create subdirectory TEMP.
- Change to TEMP, copy all files from B:\WORD to TEMP, and use the DIR command to verify the copy process. Use wildcard characters whenever possible to save keystrokes and minimize errors.
- Finally, remove the TEMP subdirectory and change back to the A> prompt. Did you remember to delete all the files in TEMP first?

**This ends Lab Exercise #6. Remove your disks when you are done, and remember, "practice is the best teacher."**

# *Chapter*

# 8

# ADVANCED COMMANDS

## ADVANCED DOS COMMANDS
☐   ASSIGN Command
     IF (Batch File Command)
     PRINT Command
     CONFIG.SYS (Configuration Command File)

# Chapter

## 8

# ADVANCED COMMANDS

*I*t may be comforting to find out that not everyone will need to know the more advanced DOS commands. One purpose of this text, however, is to acquaint you with a sampling of the advanced commands. The more you know about its capabilities, the more control you will be able to have over DOS.

## ADVANCED DOS COMMANDS

This chapter covers only those advanced DOS commands that you will most likely want to know. These selected commands are:

- The **ASSIGN** command that reroutes disk drive designators to other disk drives.
- The **IF** statement that gives your batch files flexibility by providing branching capability within a batch file.
- The **PRINT** command that allows printing concurrently with the execution of other programs or commands.
- **CONFIG.SYS**, that lets you customize your system's physical configuration and operations.

*133*

Consult your DOS manual for information on the use and operation of any other advanced commands not included in this chapter.

## ASSIGN Command (external)

**Format:** [d:]ASSIGN d:=d: [d:=d:]

The **ASSIGN** command lets the user reroute a disk drive designator. Some older application programs were designed around the assumption that the program disk would always reside in Drive A and the data disk would always be in Drive B. However, with the newer hard disk systems, it is likely that you would want both the programs and data to reside on the hard disk (Drive C). To execute those older programs, you could trick DOS by using the ASSIGN command as follows: ASSIGN A=C B=C.

This command reassigns both Drive A and Drive B to your hard disk as required by the program. To cancel drive assignments, enter the command ASSIGN without any assignments. A helpful hint: Whenever you use the ASSIGN command, incorporate it into a batch file that executes the program and automatically returns the assignments back to normal. The execution of any subsequent commands would become very confusing if you forgot to reset them.

## IF (Batch File Command)

**Format:** IF [not] condition command

When the **IF** condition specified is true, the specified command will be executed. Otherwise, the next command in the batch file will be executed. The **NOT** condition is interpreted in reverse, causing the specified command to be executed if the condition is false.

The most common use of the IF statement is to give batch files the flexibility to branch, depending on the various processing conditions that can occur during execution. A **GOTO** command is normally used in the IF statement. It directs it to branch to another location of the batch file. Branch locations must be named using the colon as the first character of the name, such as :OK or :END. Branch location names can be up to 8 characters long.

Perhaps the most difficult part of using the IF statement is formulating the conditions that will cause the desired branching. These conditions can be expressed in three different ways: **EXIST** file, **ERRORLEVEL number**, or **string1 == string2** condition. The paragraphs that follow describe these conditions and their use in the IF statement.

### EXIST File Condition

If a data file required by a batch command does not exist, the EXIST file condition lets you modify further processing of that batch file. Appropriate measures can be taken to locate the correct file before proceeding. If the specified file exists, the EXIST file condition is evaluated as true and the batch file continues executing normally. The following set of batch file commands can be used to verify that a file is available before continuing:

(previous batch file statements)

```
:LOOP
IF  EXIST A:FILEA.DOC GOTO OK
PAUSE PUT CORRECT DISK IN DRIVE A
GOTO LOOP
:OK
```

(remaining batch file commands)

If A:FILEA.DOC cannot be found by DOS, the batch file will pause and direct the user to place the correct disk in Drive A. It will then branch back to the location named LOOP and resume testing for the file. Once found, the IF statement will branch around the error condition commands and begin executing the set of commands at the location named :OK.

The use of a replaceable parameter for the specified filename gives additional flexibility. For example, the IF statement in the previous example could have been: IF EXIST A:%1 GOTO OK.

### ERRORLEVEL Number Condition

The ERRORLEVEL number condition evaluates as true when the previously executed batch file command has an error condition equal to or greater than the number specified. Since error level numbers vary by application, an error level of 1 is normally used. If an error has occurred, you could direct DOS to skip to the end of the batch file without executing the remainder of the commands. For example: IF ERRORLEVEL 1 GOTO END.

This IF statement directs DOS to branch to the :END location in the batch file whenever any error has occurred. If the error level were zero, signifying no errors, it would continue normally to the next batch file command.

### *String1 == String2 Condition*

Whenever you execute a batch file with replaceable parameters, error checking is required to ensure the parameters were provided. DOS does not do any error checking automatically, but it does provide the capability for you to check for missing parameters with the string1 == string2 condition. This condition is evaluated as true when the two strings provided are identical. *The double equals sign is required.* The technique for using this condition is a little strange, however. It is best explained with an example. If a replaceable parameter is missing in a batch file, you could direct DOS to branch to another location with the following statement: IF %2J==J GOTO ERROR.

In this example, the value of the replaceable parameter (%2) is concatenated with the letter J. If %2 is not blank, then the first string could not possibly be equal to the second string. It is only when the parameter is missing that the first string (J) will be equal to the second string (J). We have chosen to use the letter J in this example, but any character would suffice. For example, this IF statement would produce the same results: IF %2@==@ GOTO ERROR.

The IF statement gives you a great deal of flexibility to control the proper execution of batch files. Perhaps you have already thought of some ways to use the IF statement in your own batch files. Additional examples of the IF statement are shown throughout the remainder of the text.

# PRINT Command (external)

Format: [d:]PRINT [/B:buffersize] [/S:timeslice] [d:]
       filename[.ext]

Normally, when you TYPE or COPY a disk file to the printer, you must wait until all printing is completed before executing another DOS command or program. When you have long documents to be printed, you can avoid lengthy delays by utilizing the **PRINT** command.

The printer is extremely slow relative to the internal speed of the computer. Thus, a small portion of the computer's resources (RAM space and CPU time) can be allocated to the print process, while the majority of the resources can be used for other processing at the same time. It is analogous to chewing gum while reading your DOS Manual. Your mind spends relatively little time directing your mouth, concentrating most of your thinking power on attempting to understand the DOS Manual.

PRINT is a RAM-resident command that gets loaded into memory when it is first executed and stays there until you reboot the system. Another program or command (that you want to run at the same time) is also loaded into RAM. DOS executes each program concurrently, allocating a defined slice of time and a buffer size to the PRINT program. The maximum time slice is 255 slices per second with a default of 8 time slices. The maximum buffer size is 32767 with a default of 512 bytes.

The PRINT command has some limitations, however. It can only be used to print the output of files stored on disk in a printable format. Unless your application programs, like word processing, can output print files to a disk, the PRINT command will be of limited help. It cannot print the output of a program currently running. In addition, you cannot change or delete a file while it is being printed, nor can you attempt to use the printer for another operation while PRINT is using the printer. Because the description of the PRINT command in this text does not cover all its capabilities, you should refer to your DOS Manual for other options. As an alternative to PRINT, you can purchase a print spooling utility program that greatly simplifies the process of concurrent printing.

*EXAMPLES OF USAGE:*

A> `PRINT /b:1024/s:64 B:Fed.txt`
(places the file FED.TXT from Drive B into a buffer of 1024 bytes, allocates 64 time slices, and prints it concurrently with another command)

A> `print fileb.doc`
(prints FILEB.DOC on the default drive while executing other processing operations, using default values for buffer size of 512 bytes and 8 time slices per second)

A> `PRINT NUL`
(clever way causing the printer to advance to top of the next page — after printing nothing, the printer executes a form feed)

## CONFIG.SYS (Configuration Command File)

**Format: (list of special commands to configure the system)**

**CONFIG.SYS**, a special file used in the last stages of the boot process, allows you to specify how your system should operate and be configured. Primarily, CONFIG.SYS allows you to control the way memory is used and to install device driver programs for controlling other devices. It is similar to a batch file in that it is a text file of commands, usually created with EDLIN or the COPY CON command. Here are the configuration commands that you are most likely to need:

**BREAK = ON** tells DOS that you want it to check for a Ctrl-C (Ctrl-Break) from the keyboard during every disk read or write operation. Normally, DOS only checks for a Ctrl-Break during keyboard, printer, or screen operations.

**BUFFERS = nn** where nn is the number of input/output buffers desired to significantly improve disk performance. By specifying a relatively high number of buffers, you tell DOS to read a larger than usual chunk of data from your disk at one time. The next time your program needs data, DOS checks to see if it is already in the RAM buffer. If it is, access is almost immediate. Because the first microcomputers had a limited amount of RAM, the DOS default is 2 buffers for the PC-XT and 3 for an AT. A recommended setting of 20 buffers will suit most circumstances. Each buffer uses 512 bytes (1/2KB) of memory. It may require some experimenting to find the most effective buffer size for your system.

**FILES = nn** where nn is the number of files that can be used at any one time by your programs. The DOS default is 8, but it is better to have at least 15, since the number of open files include the hidden files, COMMAND.COM, and any RAM-resident programs. Database applications often require 20 or more open files.

**DEVICE = x** where x represents a particular device driver file, such as **ANSI.SYS, MOUSE.SYS, DRIVER.SYS**, or **VDISK.SYS**. A device driver is a short program that tells DOS how to handle input/output from a given peripheral device, such as a keyboard, disk, or mouse. This configuration command must be supplied for each device that requires it to be installed. The following commands are often included in a CONFIG.SYS file:

```
BREAK = ON
FILES = 20
BUFFERS = 15
DEVICE = VDISK.SYS
```

**VDISK.SYS** (RAMDRIVE.SYS in MS-DOS) is a RAM-resident device driver that lets you allocate a portion of main memory as an extra disk device, often called RAM disk or "electronic disk." Access speeds in RAM are much faster than those of a hard disk, so any files loaded into RAM disk are accessed almost immediately. DOS always creates the RAM disk drive designator, normally as Drive D.

To install the RAM disk capability, available with PC-DOS 3.x, you must have VDISK.SYS included in your CONFIG.SYS file. If you want more than the default of 64KB of RAM allocated to the RAM disk, you can enter the parameter **DEVICE = VDISK.SYS 360**. In this case, 360KB of RAM (about the size of a floppy disk) would be allocated to RAM disk.

As part of your AUTOEXEC.BAT file, you should copy the various DOS commands, batch files, and programs that you expect to execute most often into the RAM disk area. For example: `COPY C:\WP\WORD.COM D:`.

But make sure your path command includes the new RAM disk drive. For example: `PATH = D:\;C:\DOS;C:\UTIL`.

It is a dangerous practice to put data files on RAM disk, since valuable data could easily be lost during power failures or surges. Be sure to save any data files you have in RAM disk to permanent disk storage with the COPY command before turning off the CPU.

# *Review Questions*

1. What is the main purpose of the IF statement in a batch file?
2. What does a GOTO statement do in a batch file?
3. How can a batch file detect a missing replaceable parameter?
4. What is meant by the term "RAM-resident program"?
5. What is the function of a print spooler?

6. What DOS command acts as a print spooler?
7. What is the purpose of the CONFIG.SYS file?
8. How is the CONFIG.SYS file typically created?
9. What is the importance of increasing the default values for the number of buffers and the number of open files in DOS?
10. What is a "device driver"?
11. What device driver is used to create a RAM disk?
12. Why might it be dangerous to load data files to RAM disk?
13. When would you likely need to use the ASSIGN command?
14. What command is used to load a mouse driver in DOS?
15. How can batch files be used to redefine DOS commands and create your own commands? (Hint: Do the DOS Lab Exercise below.)
16. How is the CONFIG.SYS file loaded by DOS?

# □ D O S   Lab   Exercise   #7

1. Rather than purchasing a utility program to search your hard disk for a particular filename, you can create your own customized batch file named **PHIND.BAT**. You would not be able to call this file FIND.BAT because entering the batch command FIND would cause DOS to execute FIND.COM. Create the following batch file without the explanatory comments:

```
ECHO OFF  (turns echo off)
IF %1@==@ GOTO ERROR (if no parameter, branches to ERROR)
CHKDSK /V | FIND "%1" (sends all filenames to filter)
GOTO END  (unconditional branch to END)
:ERROR (branching location labeled ERROR)
ECHO FILENAME PARAMETER REQUIRED (displays error message)
:END (branching location labeled END)
```

This useful batch file will direct CHKDSK to locate every filename on your hard disk and pipe it to FIND which will filter out all filenames not containing the string of characters specified by the variable parameter (%1). The IF test allows the batch file to skip over the CHKDSK and FIND operations, if no parameter was included with the batch filename (PHIND) during execution. Figure 8-1 shows you what the screen might look like if you executed PHIND.BAT, first with no parameter and then with .EXE as a parameter. Note that PHIND.BAT was created on Drive B, yet was executed with Drive A as the default drive.

This batch file could take several minutes to execute if there were many files to be piped through the FIND filter. However, just knowing you can create such a customized batch file should make this exercise beneficial.

Use the batch file on page 140 to display all files on your DOS disk with "DIS" in the filename. Since CHKDSK will pipe all filenames in uppercase letters, the PHIND parameter (DIS) must also be in uppercase.

*Figure 8-1*

*Screen Display after Executing PHIND.BAT*

```
A>B:PHIND

A>ECHO OFF
    FILENAME PARAMETER REQUIRED

A>B:PHIND .EXE

A>ECHO OFF
        A:\ATTRIB.EXE
        A:\FIND.EXE
        A:\JOIN.EXE
        A:\SHARE.EXE
        A:\SORT.EXE
        A:\SUBST.EXE

A>
```

2. Create the following batch file called **SUPERMAT.BAT** that will format a disk with the /S option and automatically copy FORMAT.COM and CHKDSK.COM to the newly formatted disk. This would be a useful program for formatting program floppy disks that are to be bootable and contain the FORMAT and CHKDSK commands. Specific application programs could then be copied onto these bootable disks. If you have a blank disk, execute this program to verify it works correctly.

```
ECHO   OFF
REM   SUPERMAT.BAT USED TO CREATE BOOTABLE DISKS
REM
CLS
FORMAT   B:/S
COPY   FORMAT.COM   B:
COPY   CHKDSK.COM   B:
DIR   B:
ECHO   END OF SUPERMAT
```

3. The SORT filter may used to sort data in either a text file or a directory listing. Since it is able to sort beginning with any column you specify, it becomes very useful when you have fixed-length records to sort. To specify a column, use the / + n option, where n represents the number of the column where you wish to begin sorting. For example, to sort a directory by filename extension, enter:

```
DIR ¦ SORT /+10
```
   (extensions begin in column 10 of a Directory listing)

This will yield a rather strange-looking directory listing since all the heading lines are included in the sort.

Create a batch file called **DATEDIR.BAT** that will sort and display a directory in chronological date-stamp sequence (by year, month, and day). This becomes a little tricky, since the date stamp is displayed in day, month, and year format (dd-mm-yy). Use the following commands:

```
ECHO  OFF
REM  DATEDIR.BAT TO DISPLAY DIR SORTED BY DATE STAMP
DIR  %1 ¦ SORT /+27 ¦ SORT /+24 ¦ SORT /+30 ¦ MORE
REM  END OF DATEDIR.BAT
```

To execute this batch file, remember to include the disk drive designator as a parameter when entering the batch file command (DATEDIR).

4. Assume for the moment that you have a system with a hard disk and only one floppy disk. You want to make a backup copy of one of your floppy disks which contains data that is not on your hard disk. Create a batch file called C:BUP.BAT that will facilitate this process, one you anticipate performing often. ECHO should not be turned off while the batch file is being executed. This will let you see the batch file steps during its execution. The batch file should contain the statements at the top of the next page.

```
REM  BACKUP A FLOPPY DISK ONTO ANOTHER FLOPPY USING
REM  A ONE FLOPPY, SINGLE HARD DISK SYSTEM.
REM
MD   C:\TEMP8765
REM  INSERT ORIGINAL FLOPPY IN DRIVE A:
PAUSE
COPY  A:*.*  C:\TEMP8765
REM  INSERT BLANK FLOPPY IN DRIVE A:
PAUSE
FORMAT  A:
COPY  C:\TEMP8765\*.*  A:
REM
REM  RESPOND WITH "Y" TO THE "ARE YOU SURE" PROMPT
REM
DEL  C:\TEMP8765\*.*
RD   C:\TEMP8765
REM  END OF BACKUP
DIR  A:/P
```

If you have a hard disk system, test this batch file to make sure it works. Otherwise, you could use Drive B in place of Drive C to execute this batch file. The subdirectory name TEMP8765 was chosen because it is highly unlikely that it already exists on Drive C.

5. If you are currently connected on-line to a printer, you can complete this portion of the exercise. Otherwise, just read through it and use your imagination to see how it would execute.

Without special software, concurrent processing with DOS (Version 3.x) is limited to two operations at a time. This can be accomplished in DOS by executing one operation while printing from a print queue. To do this, enter PRINT B:TEST3.DIR and identify the printing device (PRN) when prompted by DOS.

Just as soon as printing begins, enter DIR ¦ SORT ¦ MORE. DOS will overlap execution of these operations, using somewhat less time to finish the concurrent processing than if the two commands were not overlapped (executed separately).

6. Bonus exercise (requires application of prior learning):

- Assume you will be leaving your computer for a short time and you want to discourage novice users from using your system. By entering ECHO OFF followed by CLS, your screen will become blank with just the flashing cursor. Experiment with this by running some commands without any prompt displayed. Then restore the prompt by turning echo back on.
- Use EDLIN to create a CONFIG.SYS file on Drive B that will provide for up to 20 files and 15 buffers in DOS, allocate 256K of RAM for a RAM disk, and set Break ON. Your CONFIG.SYS file should look something like this if you are using PC-DOS (Version 3.x):

```
FILES = 20
BUFFERS = 15
DEVICE = VDISK.SYS 256
BREAK = ON
```

The order of the CONFIG.SYS entries is irrelevant.

**This is the end of Lab Exercise #7. Best wishes learning more DOS!**

# SUMMARY OF DOS COMMANDS

| DOS Command | Covered in Text | Brief Description of Command |
|---|---|---|
| APPEND | No | Sets a search path for data files. |
| ASSIGN | Yes | Assigns a disk drive letter to another. |
| ATTRIB | Yes | Sets/displays attributes of a file. |
| BACKUP | Yes | Backs up files from disk. |
| BREAK | Yes | Sets Ctrl-Break check. |
| CD (CHDIR) | Yes | Changes directories. |
| CHKDSK | Yes | Checks for file fragmentation on a disk. |
| CLS | Yes | Clears the screen. |
| COMMAND | Yes | Supplies internal DOS commands. |
| COMP | Yes | Compares two files for differences. |
| COPY | Yes | Copies specified files. |
| DATE | Yes | Displays and sets the system date. |
| DEL | Yes | Deletes (erases) specified files. |
| DIR | Yes | Displays directory entries. |
| DISKCOMP | Yes | Compares two disks. |
| DISKCOPY | Yes | Makes an exact copy of a disk. |
| EDLIN | Yes | Executes the DOS line editor. |
| ERASE | Yes | Identical to DEL command. |

| DOS Command | Covered in Text | Brief Description of Command |
|---|---|---|
| EXE2BIN | No | Converts executable files to binary. |
| FASTOPEN | No | Improves hard disk performance. |
| FDISK | Yes | Partitions a hard disk for DOS. |
| FIND | Yes | Searches for a given string of text. |
| FORMAT | Yes | Formats a disk to receive DOS files. |
| GRAFTABL | No | Loads a table of graphics characters. |
| GRAPHICS | No | Prepares DOS for printing graphics. |
| JOIN | No | Joins a disk drive to a pathname. |
| LABEL | Yes | Labels a disk. |
| MD (MKDIR) | Yes | Makes a directory. |
| MODE | No | Modifies system parameters. |
| MORE | Yes | Displays output one screen at a time. |
| PATH | Yes | Sets a command search path. |
| PRINT | Yes | Prints a file concurrently. |
| PROMPT | Yes | Assigns the system prompt. |
| RECOVER | Yes | Recovers a bad disk or file. |
| REPLACE | No | Facilitates updating of files. |
| RENAME (REN) | Yes | Renames a file. |
| RESTORE | Yes | Restores previously backed up files. |
| RD (RMDIR) | Yes | Removes a directory. |
| SELECT | No | Selects keyboard and country conventions. |
| SET | No | Sets one string value to another. |
| SHARE | No | Installs file sharing and locking. |
| SORT | Yes | Sorts data forward or backward. |
| SUBST | No | Substitutes a string for a pathname. |
| SYS | Yes | Transfers DOS hidden files to a disk. |
| TIME | Yes | Displays and sets the system time. |
| TREE | Yes | Displays directories and filenames. |
| TYPE | Yes | Displays contents of a file. |
| VER | Yes | Displays the DOS version number. |
| VERIFY | Yes | Verifies all writes to a disk. |
| VOL | Yes | Displays the disk volume label. |
| XCOPY | No | Expanded version of the COPY command. |

# DOS Batch File Commands

| Command | Covered in Text | Brief Description of Command |
| --- | --- | --- |
| **ECHO** | Yes | Sets the batch file echo feature on/off. |
| **FOR** | No | Command for repetitive looping. |
| **GOTO** | Yes | Command for branching. |
| **IF** | Yes | Command for conditional branching. |
| **PAUSE** | Yes | Pauses for input in a batch file. |
| **REM** | Yes | Provides for remarks in a batch file. |
| **SHIFT** | No | Increases the number of replaceable parameters. |

# DOS EDLIN Commands

| Command | Covered in Text | Brief Description of Command |
| --- | --- | --- |
| **#** | Yes | Edits a given line. |
| **A** | No | Appends lines. |
| **C** | Yes | Copies lines. |
| **D** | Yes | Deletes lines. |
| **E** | Yes | Ends editing and saves the file. |
| **I** | Yes | Inserts lines. |
| **L** | Yes | Lists lines. |
| **M** | Yes | Moves lines. |
| **P** | No | Pages text (scrolling). |
| **Q** | Yes | Quits editing without saving the file. |
| **R** | Yes | Replaces text in lines. |
| **S** | Yes | Searches for text. |
| **T** | Yes | Transfers text from other files. |
| **W** | No | Writes a partial file to main memory for editing. |

# B

# UTILITY SUPPORT PROGRAMS

*F*rustration with DOS is a fairly common occurrence. This frustration is caused by misplaced files, awkward commands, and a general lack of capabilities. Yet for under $100, users can supplement DOS and overcome many of its shortcomings.

Numerous utility support programs are available that make DOS easier to use and/or extend its capabilities. Usually menu-driven, they are relatively user-friendly. Some programs are complete DOS **command shells** that execute DOS commands and their options with menu selections. These are specifically designed to guide users through the process of executing DOS commands, especially in the area of disk file management. Other utility support programs extend the capabilities of DOS. In the opinion of many users, these programs provide capabilities and a structure that should have been included in DOS in the first place. Some examples are the ability to recover lost or deleted files, find hard disk files more easily, and improved backup and restore operations.

Some utility support programs are RAM-resident, which means that they stay in RAM until you need them. They generally can be executed with a simple combination of keystrokes, even while you are using another program. These programs are also referred to as terminate and stay resident or **TSR** for short.

Using TSR software carries some dangers, especially if you are using more than one TSR program. TSR programs can take up valuable space that might be better allocated to the main program. Some programs take over control of the keyboard so tightly that they don't allow you access to call up your TSR programs. Finally, loading TSR programs in the wrong sequence can cause your system to lock up. This problem can often be resolved by shuffling the order.

It is not always easy finding a utility program that best meets your specific needs. This appendix lists just a small sampling of some of the more common and useful utility programs, along with a brief description of each. Because software prices vary significantly depending on the time and location of purchase, these utility programs are listed in two groups: those that typically cost under $50 (including discount prices) and those that typically cost between $50–$100. Software developers are continually improving the features offered and their prices historically drop as sales increase. Therefore, the listings that follow are, at best, to be used as a guide as to what types of general support programs are available.

One word of caution: Beware of utility programs that you download from an electronic bulletin board or that are given to you by a friend. They may contain a **"computer virus"** that, when loaded to your system and executed, could cause major problems, such as destroying all your disk files.

# A SAMPLING OF DOS UTILITIES FOR UNDER $50

| *Program Name* | *Major Program Features* |
| --- | --- |
| **Automenu** | Powerful personal menu system. |
| **COPYIIPC** | Backs up protected software and allows it to be executed from hard disk. |
| **Cruise Control** | Keyboard accelerator, autodimmer for the monitor. |
| **dirWorks** | DOS shell with good hard disk management routines. |
| **Disk Optimizer** | Restores fragmented files, includes disk analyzer. |
| **DoubleDOS** | Supplements DOS, runs two partitions concurrently. |
| **GOfer** | Searches hard disk files for data. |

| *Program Name* | *Major Program Features* |
| --- | --- |
| **Norton Commander** | Popular DOS shell. |
| **Norton Utilities** | Extensive file management and file recovery. |
| **PC Tools Deluxe** | Disk file management and recovery, desktop manager, and backup facilities. |
| **ProComm Plus** | Powerful communications program. |
| **Q-DOS** | Friendly shell using sorted and tagged files. |
| **SideKick** | Extensive desktop organizer. |
| **SuperKey** | Keyboard redefinition, macro generation, and keyboard lock. |
| **XTREE** | DOS shell and disk management system, good graphic display of a tree structure. |

## A SAMPLING OF DOS UTILITIES ($50–$100)

| *Program Name* | *Major Program Features* |
| --- | --- |
| **1 Dir Plus** | DOS shell with numerous disk management routines. |
| **Crosstalk** | Excellent communications facilities. |
| **DesQview** | Excellent multitasking DOS shell with windows. |
| **DOS2ools** | Numerous utility programs that extend DOS, including security, undelete, and print spooler. |
| **Fastback** | Fast and friendly disk backup. |
| **Nathan's Utilities** | DOS shell with numerous utilities, disk optimizer. |
| **Norton Utilities Advanced** | Menu-driven advanced file management, including extensive file recovery. |
| **Microsoft Windows** | Mouse-directed DOS shell with multitasking and good integration capabilities. |

# INDEX